# ENGLISH LANGUAGE
## for AQA B

Ron Norman
Anne Watkiss

Heinemann

Heinemann Educational Publishers,
Halley Court, Jordan Hill, Oxford OX2 8EJ
A division of Reed Educational & Professional Publishing Ltd

OXFORD  MELBOURNE  AUCKLAND
JOHANNESBURG  BLANTYRE  GABORONE
IBADAN  PORTSMOUTH NH (USA)  CHICAGO

First published 2000

2004  2003  2002  2001  2000
10  9  8  7  6  5  4  3  2

ISBN 0 435 13227 X

## Acknowledgements

The publishers would like to thank the following for permission to use copyright material:

*Sociolinguistics: An Introduction* by Peter Trudgill (Penguin Books 1974), Fourth Edition 2000. Copyright Peter Trudgill 1974, 1995, 2000. With permission of Penguin Books Ltd; CDefender advertisement with kind permission of OptiDisk UK Ltd; 'Language Buffs Launch New SOS' by Vanessa Thorpe, with permission of the *Guardian*; Maps from *Word Maps: A Dialect Atlas of England* with permission of Dr Clive Upton; 'Children using geatt words' by David Gow, with permission of the *Guardian*; 'Listen Mr Oxford don' by Jon Agard with permission of Serpent's Tail; Map from *The Cambridge Encyclopedia of the English Language* by David Crystal (CUP 1995) with permission of Cambridge University Press; Colman's advertisement with kind permission of Van den Burgh Foods; Extract from *The Secret Diary of Adrian Mole, Aged 13 3/4* by Sue Townsend, with permission of Random House Group Ltd; 'Snow-White and the Seven Dwarfs' by Roald Dahl from *Revolting Rhymes*, with permission of David Higham Associates; 'In Very Poor Taste', Leader article in the *Guardian* 30/9/99, with permission of the *Guardian*; 'RSPCA Killer Pack' with permission of Countrywide Periodical Publishing Ltd; 'Wild Wild West' with permission of *Live and Kicking* Magazine; 'Tiny Walkman that turns your computer into a record store', *Daily Mail*, with permission of Solo Syndication; 'Vikings' from Encyclopedia Britannica, with permission of Britannica.co.uk Ltd; 'How to Earn as Much as a Man' Adapted from *Company* September 1999 © National Magazine Company.

The publishers have made every effort to trace the copyright holders, but if they have inadvertently overlooked any, they will be pleased to make the necessary arrangements at the first opportunity.

The authors would like to thank the students of Prior Pursglove College and Judy Carrick for their data and suggested text extracts; the students at Bury College and Ben Dowson for text extracts; Mr James Martin; Sue Lester and Mike Jago for advice and suggestions; Geraldine Norman for additional research and suggestions.

Typeset by TechType, Abingdon, Oxon

Printed and bound by Bath Press in the UK

# Contents

# Introduction

This book will support and stimulate you as you embark on the new AS English Language courses available from September 2000. You will rapidly discover how fascinating and challenging the study of language at this level can be, particularly if you use the materials in this book to sustain your learning. If you are following the AQA English Language A specification, you may recognise that we follow the structure and module titles of that course – though we also hope the book will be of value if you are taking one of the other specifications.

Like all the new AS courses, English Language AS consists of three modules. You may be taught and then tested on these modules one after another; alternatively, your teachers may decide to present elements of all three throughout the year and enter you for all three modules together. For example, although 'Original Writing' is presented here as a separate and final module for assessment purposes (as in the AQA specification), many original writing opportunities arise from the work covered in the other two modules. However, you will probably find it best to start by working through Module 1, 'Introduction to the Study of Language', as it establishes the basis for many of the ideas and linguistic terms that arise in the other two modules.

For the sake of clarity, this book covers the three modules in separate parts, but where you see one of these symbols

there is a link to work covered in one of the other modules.

You will also see signposts that highlight links to elements of the A2 course. Although some aspects of the A2 course introduce new topics and approaches, in many other ways it builds on your learning during the AS course so these links will be useful. When you have completed all three modules and taken the AS examination, many of you will opt to continue your English language studies by moving on to that course.

## Using this book

The book uses several different types of text:

- *teaching text* that introduces ideas and approaches, and explains and comments on linguistic material; study these sections before embarking on any of the activities

- *data and extracts* composed of passages, excerpts and other examples of language in use; these form the raw material of your study, so read and respond to them carefully

- *instructions or suggestions for activities*, which are usually one of the following: data gathering or research, group discussion or individual work

- *commentaries* and answers to the activities for you to compare with the outcomes of your own work; try to resist reading these before completing the activities for yourself, and remember that the commentary is not necessarily the only 'correct' response or analysis – differences between your suggestions and ours may provoke fruitful discussion

## Linguistic terminology and the glossaries

As you work through this book you will be introduced to a number of specialist linguistic terms; you should gradually become more comfortable with using these in your discussions and analysis of language. The first time these terms appear they are printed in bold text. Sometimes they are introduced in the commentaries rather than in the teaching text, because we have resorted to technical terminology only when linguistic explorations demand it.

These terms also appear in the glossary at the end of the book, but you are strongly advised to develop your own personal glossary in a notebook, along with your own definition and some personal examples for each term. These will then serve as a useful revision source when you prepare for the module examinations.

## Assessment Objectives

Whichever English language specification you are following, the course has been designed to enable students to meet the same set of Assessment Objectives. These define the skills and knowledge that you must demonstrate to the examiners in your assessments.

| The syllabus says you have to . . . | In other words, . . . |
|---|---|
| communicate clearly the knowledge, understanding and insight appropriate to the study of language, using appropriate terminology and accurate and coherent written expression | whatever you write should be clearly expressed, with a high standard of accuracy in spelling and grammar, and you should make use of specialist technical terms where this helps to define ideas and features of language precisely |
| demonstrate expertise and accuracy in writing for a variety of specific purposes and audiences, drawing on knowledge of linguistic features to explain and comment on choices made | you must show that you can choose to write in different styles according to the needs of different purposes and readerships, and that you can explain how and why you have deliberately adjusted your use of language to suit the people and context you are writing for |

| The syllabus says you have to . . . | In other words, . . . |
|---|---|
| know and use key features of frameworks for the systematic study of spoken and written English | in your analysis of texts you must put into the practice some of the theoretical models and ideas about language that you learn at different points in the course. This means more than simply using a 'common sense' approach |
| understand, discuss and explore concepts and issues relating to language in use | as in the previous objective, you must show that you understand some important ideas about language and the factors that influence how it is used |
| distinguish, describe and interpret variation in the meanings and forms of spoken and written language according to context | you must look very closely and in detail at different kinds of text, and explain in depth what is meant and implied |

**Assessment Objectives for AS English Language**

At the start of each module you will see how varying numbers of marks are attached to the different Assessment Objectives, so during your preparation it is important that you know which objectives you must meet. To help you, we relate the weightings and the various topics and activities to the individual objectives.

It is vital that you check your own work against the Objectives to ensure that you meet the requirements for each part of the examination. Teachers must be aware of how the work being done relates to the Objectives and the relative weighting they have in any given part of the specification.

A fuller discussion of the Assessment Objectives appears in the 'Preparing for the Examination' section towards the end of each module.

# Key Skills

The activities suggested in the AS modules offer numerous opportunities to produce evidence of the attainment of all the Key Skills. Where such opportunities arise, we indicate this with the Key Skills symbol e.g. **C3.1A**

| Communication | |
|---|---|
| C3.1a | Contribute to discussions |
| C3.1b | Make a presentation |
| C3.2 | Read and synthesise information |
| C3.3 | Write different types of document |
| **Working with others** | |
| WO3.1 | Plan the activity |
| WO3.2 | Work towards agreed objectives |
| WO3.3 | Review the activity |
| **Improving own learning and performance** | |
| LP3.1 | Agree and plan targets |
| LP3.2 | Seek feedback and support |
| LP3.3 | Review progress |

**Definitions of Key Skills indicated**

This map indicates which topics or skills receive explicit coverage in each module. Elsewhere, the application of previous work may be assumed or implicit in the exercises and activities. Modules 1–3 are covered in English Language AS; Modules 4–6 are covered in English Language A2.

| | Introduction to the study of language | Language in social contexts | Original writing | Language development | Language investigation | Editorial writing |
|---|---|---|---|---|---|---|
| Classifying and describing language | ✓ | ✓ | ✓ | ✓ | ✓ | ✓ |
| Variation in audience, register and purposes | ✓ | ✓ | ✓ | | ✓ | ✓ |
| Levels of linguistic description | ✓ | | | | ✓ | |
| Looking at word classes | ✓ | | | ✓ | ✓ | |
| Morphology: the grammar of words | ✓ | | | ✓ | ✓ | |
| Syntax: the grammar of sentences | ✓ | | | ✓ | ✓ | |
| Comparing speech and writing | ✓ | | | ✓ | ✓ | |
| Looking at language functions | ✓ | ✓ | | ✓ | ✓ | |
| The sounds of English: phonemes and the phonetic alphabet | ✓ | | | ✓ | | |
| The sounds of English: prosodic features | ✓ | | | ✓ | | |
| Sounds and spellings | ✓ | | | ✓ | ✓ | |
| Analysing conversation | ✓ | ✓ | | ✓ | ✓ | |
| Gender and language | | ✓ | | | ✓ | |
| Power and language | | ✓ | | | ✓ | |
| Social class and language | | ✓ | | | ✓ | |
| Looking at accent, dialect, Standard English and received pronunciation | ✓ | ✓ | | | ✓ | |
| Historical change in language | | ✓ | | ✓ | ✓ | |
| Contemporary change in language | | ✓ | | ✓ | ✓ | |
| Language acquisition | | | | ✓ | ✓ | |
| Original writing | | | ✓ | | | |
| Writing a commentary | | | ✓ | | | |
| Approaches to investigating language data | | | | | ✓ | |
| Stylistic analysis of data and texts | ✓ | ✓ | | | ✓ | |
| Editorial writing | | | | | | ✓ |
| Cohesion and coherence in language | | | | | ✓ | ✓ |
| Examining and preparing source material for rewriting | | | | | | ✓ |

# MODULE (1) Introduction to the Study of Language

This module counts for 35% of the AS qualification, or $17^1/_2$% of the total A Level marks.

## ASSESSMENT OBJECTIVES

The skills and knowledge that you develop in this module, and that will be tested in the examination you take at the end of it, are defined by the examination board's Assessment Objectives. These require that you:

- communicate clearly the knowledge, understanding and insight appropriate to the study of language, using appropriate terminology and accurate and coherent written expression
  (10% of the final AS mark; 5% of the final A Level mark)

- know and use key features of frameworks for the systematic study of spoken and written English
  (10% of the final AS mark; 5% of the final A Level mark)

- understand, discuss and explore concepts and issues relating to language in use
  (5% of the final AS mark; $2^1/_2$% of the final A Level mark)

- distinguish, describe and interpret variation in the meanings and forms of spoken and written language according to context
  (10% of the final AS mark; 5% of the final A Level mark)

## Starting to explore

English is the language that you grew up with, and you have become skilled at using it in many situations. What's more, if you have committed yourself to studying it on your AS/A Level course, you've also probably proved to a GCSE examiner that you are rather good at reading, writing, speaking and listening.

The remarkable thing is just how automatic all of this has been. When composing that special letter of application for a job, or a tricky English assignment, we may be conscious of choosing our words carefully, but as native speakers we normally don't have to think very hard about the language we are using – there isn't time!

It's rather like learning to drive a car. At first, you'll probably find that it's difficult to co-ordinate the actions of steering, signalling, checking mirrors, changing gears, reading road signs and so on, but you soon stop thinking consciously about the complicated series of actions needed to get the car from A to B. What's more, most people become drivers without having to learn about the mechanics of the engine, or the intricacies of gearbox and transmission, or the fuel-injection system.

However, during your AS/A Level English Language course, as well as becoming a better 'driver' – developing your own skills as a user of English – you will investigate the workings of the language itself. You will become aware of the unconscious processes that are going on all the time when we use language, as we 'lift the bonnet' and examine just what makes language 'go'.

## The 'science' of language study

It is almost as if we need to consider language study as a kind of science. If you are taking a science subject, you will be familiar with certain methods of study such as:

- collecting and examining data (observing experiments, collecting specimens)

- describing, classifying and analysing data using diagrams, measurements and calculations

- testing different ideas about how things work

These same activities are the basis of your English Language studies. The 'data' can be found anywhere and everywhere – wherever the spoken or written word is used. You will learn how to describe language precisely and to classify it in many different ways, developing an appropriate terminology for the purpose. As in science, you will also consider possible explanations for your discoveries – even if you cannot expect to achieve absolute certainty or agreement in your answers.

The aim of your English Language course – and this book – is to help you develop an informed understanding of our language and to become an increasingly accomplished user of it. To achieve this, you need to become something of a linguistic explorer.

## A question of language

### ACTIVITY 1                                    C3.1A

Let's start by looking at the kinds of question that will drive our linguistic explorations forwards. The issues you begin to explore here underpin much of the work that you will do throughout your AS/A Level course.

The following language notes and queries arose from a series of interviews with English students. Read the queries and share with your classmates your first reactions to each one. Then, through discussion, try to reach agreement about an answer within your group.

After you have reported back to the class, compare your responses with the brief commentaries offered on page 46.

## A ANN, 17

Why do people's accents, and even the words and phrases they use, vary so much – and is it true that some kinds of English are 'better' than others?

## B MICHAEL, 19

Which came first, speech or writing – and which is more important?

## C AYUMI, 16

When I'm at work I have to watch what I say and talk to customers in the way I've been trained to do. Out with my friends, it's different – we have our own set of words which we use all the time and if you didn't know them you probably wouldn't understand what we were on about half the time. Is this normal?

## D GEORGE, 25

I saw a science fiction film in which instead of checking fingerprints, a computer could identify any human being just by analysing the way they talked. So, is it true that we have a sort of linguistic fingerprint – and would this also work with an extract of something which we wrote?

## E KIBRIA, 22

What I don't understand when I look at Shakespeare's language, or even hear clips from old radio and TV shows, is why English has changed so much – and who makes it happen?

## F JANET, 30

I always hated languages at school – we had to do French and German – and I always struggled with them. Now I've got kids of my own, I'm amazed by how easily they pick up English without really seeming to try! Why is my 4-year-old so much better at language than me?

## Keeping a personal glossary

Throughout this book, you will be introduced to – and encouraged to use – terminology suitable for the precise description of what you find. Remember: the Assessment Objectives require you to use 'appropriate terminology'. Although the glossary at the end of this book should help, it is a good idea to build up a personal glossary of your own.

Even before you started your AS studies, you had a working vocabulary of the language we use to talk about language. Basic terms such as 'word', 'sentence' and 'paragraph' are all part of this vocabulary.

### ACTIVITY 2

Take an exercise book and allow a couple of pages for each letter of the alphabet. List under each letter any language terms (such as 'word', 'sentence', 'full stop') that you already know. You'll probably be able to list many terms already.

As the course develops, add new terms, definitions and examples to each page as and when they arise.

## Language all around us

The scope of English Language study at A Level is extremely wide. As explorers and students of language, we can start by making ourselves aware of the sheer variety of the language that we consume or produce as a matter of routine. This variety is the raw material for our investigations and explorations.

### ACTIVITY 3                                                    C3.1A/B

Consider the four linguistic activities of Listening, Speaking, Reading and Writing. Allocate each of them to one quarter of a large circle, as in the figure.

In each quadrant, list as many examples as you can of different kinds of language activity in which you participate in a typical week. Aim to include at least half a dozen different activities in each quadrant.

For example, under Speaking you might start by listing:

- on the phone to friends

- explaining the school/college day to parents

- social chat over lunch

Once you have listed your examples, classify them in any way you think is helpful. For example, you might describe both 'on the phone to friends' and 'social chat over lunch' as 'Informal chat'.

After briefly presenting your findings to the rest of the class, compare your results with the commentary on page 47. (page 47)

## Looking at varieties: describing and classifying

Having reminded ourselves of the huge variety of language all around us, we must now look more closely at a range of examples of language in use. Throughout your English Language course, you will be encouraged to collect and describe 'data' – that is, specimens of speech and writing – and to explore ways in which these specimens can be compared with or distinguished from each other.

The texts and activities in this section introduce you to the process of description and classification.

### ACTIVITY 4      C3.1A/B

On the next page there are nine texts, Extracts A–I. (The word 'text' is used throughout this book to describe any piece of language in either written or spoken form.) Read each text carefully.

In groups, agree how to organise the texts into five groups, linking them by identifying some aspect that they have in common. Record your findings in the form of a table:

| Linked texts | Features in common |
|---|---|
|  |  |
|  |  |
|  |  |
|  |  |
|  |  |

Present and explain your findings to the class, then compare them with the commentary on page 47. (page 47)

## EXTRACT A

Right – you have a sheet in front of you – wait a minute I'll get you one – on it – have a look now please – on it – there's a list of the characters we looked at on Friday – look at the paragraph underneath – look at the paragraph underneath – what I want you to do please – is to ensure that you have a pen or pencil available to you – and that as we learn anything about any of the characters – you add any relevant information onto the sheet

## EXTRACT B

There were times – if you felt in good fettle – we used to see who could hoy a ball furthest – it was a nice canny game an all but sometimes – windows used to get brocken – and another thing – in them days people were lucky if they had indoor netties – and it was bloody murder if you wanted to gan to the toilet in the middle of the neet

## EXTRACT C

We joined the ship on Wednesday morning, the 10th of April, and had boat drill and proceeded at 12 o'clock. We called at Cherbourg and Queenstown. On Sunday it came in rather cold, Sunday afternoon. On Sunday night at about a quarter to 12, I was on the watch below and turned in, when there was suddenly a noise like cable running out, like a ship dropping anchor. There was not any shock at all.

## EXTRACT D

Come live with me and be my love,
And we will all the pleasures prove,
That hills and valleys, dale and fields,
And all the craggy mountains yields.

## EXTRACT E

To upgrade from an earlier version of Windows

1.  Insert Setup Disk I in a floppy disk drive or your Windows CD-ROM in a CD-ROM drive.
2.  In File Manager or Program Manager, click File, and then click Run.

3. Type the drive letter, followed by a colon (:) and a backslash (\), and the word setup. For example:

    a:\setup

Note that if you install from a CD-ROM, precede the word 'setup' with **win95\.**

4. Follow the instructions on your screen. Click Next to continue through the Setup process.

## EXTRACT F

A: Tanya from West Shields on line 2. Hi Tanya.

T: Hi Alan.

A: Helloa, the best and the worst from you.

T: The best for me was going to Canada – em – 4 years ago to see an adopted sister.

A: Right – which –

T: I'd never met before.

A: Which lump of Canada was it?

T: Er, Toronto and then I flew on to Winnipeg.

A: Oh great. I mean what's – you always get the impression that Canada's – like – just massive, this immense country. What –

T: It is.
A: What's it actually like?

## EXTRACT G

They went to sea in a Sieve, they did,
    In a Sieve they went to sea:
    In spite of all their friends could say,
On a winter's morn, on a stormy day,

    In a Sieve they went to sea!
And when the Sieve turned round and round,
And everyone cried, 'You'll all be drowned!'
They called aloud, 'Our Sieve ain't big,
'But we don't care a button! we don't care a fig!
    'In a Sieve we'll go to sea!'

## EXTRACT H

From the beginning all men by nature were created alike, and our bondage or servitude came in by the unjust oppression of naughty men. And therefore I exhort you to consider that now the time is come, appointed to us by God, in which ye may (if ye will) cast off the yoke of bondage, and recover liberty. I counsel you therefore to bethink yourselves, and take good hearts unto you, that after the manner of a good husband that tilleth his ground, and riddeth out thereof such evil weeds as choke and destroy the good corn, you may destroy first the great lords of the realm, and after, the judges and lawyers, and questmongers, and all others who have undertaken to be against the common.

## EXTRACT I

'Why, look yer 'ere.' said the miner, showing the shoulders of his singlet. 'It's a bit dry now, but it's wet as a clout with sweat even yet. Feel it.'

'Goodness!' cried Mrs Morel. 'Mr Heaton doesn't want to feel your nasty singlet.'

The clergyman put out his hand gingerly.

'No, perhaps he doesn't,' said Morel; 'but it's all come out of *me*, whether or not. An' iv'ry day alike my singlet's wringin' wet. 'Aven't you got a drink, Missis, for a man when he comes home barkled up from the pit?'

## Collecting your own data

### ACTIVITY 5

Go back to the four headings you used to classify examples of language use on page 4: Listening, Speaking, Reading and Writing. For any one of these, collect your own examples of six of the uses of language you suggested there.

For Reading and Writing, you should be able to find examples of texts easily; for Speaking and Listening, you can start by making brief recordings of broadcast media. However, for examples of 'real' conversational speech you need to make tape recordings – but always follow the guidelines below:

**Guidelines for recording and writing down 'live' speech**

- Seek permission from any participants before arranging to tape record conversations
- Offer to wipe or destroy your tape if the participants object to the content afterwards
- Let your recorder run for long enough to allow people to become less self-conscious about being recorded
- Write down a short but accurate extract of what is on the tape

Such a record of spoken language is called a **transcript**. Don't try to use conventional punctuation – indicate pauses with the symbol (.) and use overlapping slash lines (//) to show where two or more people are speaking at once. Don't censor or correct the speech – represent any pauses, hesitations and 'bad' language.

Use the example on page 60 as a model for your transcripts.

### ACTIVITY 6                                                                C3.1A/B

Using the data you assembled during Activity 5, carry out a similar matching and pairing exercise as on page 5 and again record your findings in a table. This time, use the 'Commentary' column if you need to add an explanation of your pairing.

| Matched pairs | Linguistic features in common | Commentary (topic, purpose, audience, etc.) |
|---|---|---|
|  |  |  |
|  |  |  |
|  |  |  |

Present and explain your findings to the class.

## ACTIVITY 7

First, make sure you have read the commentary to Activity 4 on page 47, which introduces some important linguistic terminology.

Then, for any one of your pairs of texts from Activity 6, complete this chart:

| Text | Topic | Mode | Purpose | Audience | Register | Chron-ology | Genre | Dialect |
|---|---|---|---|---|---|---|---|---|
| | What is it about? | Spoken or written? | Why was it said or written? | Who is it for? | Formal/informal? Typical vocab-ulary? | When was it produced? | Report, story, poem, letter, advert, etc.? | Standard English, regional variation, etc.? |
| Text 1 | | | | | | | | |
| Text 2 | | | | | | | | |

## Linguistic fingerprints: describing language

Although it helps to be able to label examples of language in this way, we must now consider how to describe more precisely the way a writer or speaker uses language.

In other words, we'll attempt to understand the distinctive 'fingerprint' that makes a particular kind of writing or speech the way it is. This will involve us in an activity called stylistic analysis.

## ACTIVITY 8                                    C3.1A

Let's start by looking at one of our earlier texts, Extract D on page 6. It is clearly:

- a love poem (topic, genre)

- fairly formal and set in the country (register)

- written at some time in the past (chronology)

- persuasive (purpose)

With your group, pick out aspects of the language used in the poem that enable us to recognise these features. Record your observations as a 'spider diagram' before comparing them with the commentary on page 48.

## Stylistic analysis: using a framework

In Activity 8 you may have produced a successful snapshot of a text, but in stylistic analysis we cannot rely on being able to spot key features merely by chance. As linguistic scientists and explorers, we need to look systematically at language, asking a methodical series of questions about language as we investigate it.

This is what is meant in the Assessment Objective, to 'know and use key features of frameworks for the systematic study of spoken and written English'. So what are those key questions?

We can understand the points made in the commentary on Activity 8 (page 48) as if they were answers to several key questions that form the basis of our study of language.

## ACTIVITY 9

The table sets out these key questions and adds a 'key terms' column to enable you to flag up important linguistic terminology for later reference.

Study the examples drawn from Extract D (page 6), then fill in the rest of the table with your answers to the key questions for one of the other texts.

Make yourself familiar with this framework and its key questions; it is the basis of much of the work that follows in this module. Later sections and activities explore it more fully. Once you are familiar with it, you can use it to define the key stylistic features of any text you come across.

### Stylistic fingerprints: a framework of key questions

| Key question | In other words . . . | Example: Extract D | Example: other text | Key terms for future study |
|---|---|---|---|---|
| How is the text organised? | Does it have a clear beginning/middle/end? Is it a list? Is it a series of steps? | Starts with an invitation . . . will lead to the promised result – pleasures | | discourse structure |
| What does it look like on the page? | Is it set out in columns? Paragraphs? Verses? Are its sections numbered or titled? Does it include panels of text or diagrams? Does it use different typefaces, type sizes? | A verse of short, regular lines | | form; layout; graphology |

| Key question | In other words . . . | Example: Extract D | Example: other text | Key terms for future study |
|---|---|---|---|---|
| What kinds of sentences does it use, and how are they constructed? | How many sentences are statements? Questions? Commands? Exclamations? Are the sentences long, short or a mixture? Does their construction seem basic or complicated? Does the text use complete, 'correct' sentences or some abbreviated ones? Are there examples of unusual word order? | A command, followed by a promise or prediction. Mainly 'normal', but some unusual word order ('we will all the pleasures prove') | | sentence function/ length/structure |
| What kinds of vocabulary and phrases does it use? | What proportion of the words convey facts or opinions? Is the language emotional or detached? Does it seem personal or impersonal, simple or sophisticated, formal/neutral/ informal? Does it include words that belong to a particular subject or theme? Or words that are specialist, technical, literary or old-fashioned? Are there any non-standard or regional expressions? Is language being used in its literal sense – or does it use similes and/or metaphors and other expressions? | Personal words ('you' and 'we'). Quite simple words ('come') with parts of the country landscape ('hills', 'dales', etc.). 'Prove' used in a different, old-fashioned sense | | colloquialism; slang; archaism; jargon; dialect; metaphor; figurative language; idioms; register; semantic fields; word classes |

| Key question | In other words . . . | Example: Extract D | Example: other text | Key terms for future study |
|---|---|---|---|---|
| What is distinctive about the spellings or sounds used? | Is the text generally orthodox, or are there examples of unusual spellings or punctuation? Does the speech have a non-regional ('BBC'), 'posh' or regional accent? Are there any noticeable patterns in the sounds/spellings? | Rhyme at the ends of lines. Regular rhythm | | orthography; received pronunciation (RP); rhythm; alliteration; assonance |

## Using the stylistics framework: levels of description

The stylistics framework examines language on five levels:

1 discourse structure

2 discourse layout, form and graphology

3 sentences: length, construction and function

4 words and phrases

5 sounds and spellings

Let's explore each of these levels more fully.

## 1 Discourse structure

What do we mean by the structure of a piece of language? We can usually recognise what holds everyday objects together: a building, for example, generally consists of a set of foundations, and an interconnecting series of load-bearing walls, beams and girders. Just as different buildings – houses, churches, stadiums – have different structures, so uses of language have their own distinctive structures too.

There are many different ways in which texts and speech can be organised, but some common structures do occur frequently. You will certainly be able to recognise and identify examples of these. We'll start with the structures of stories.

### Four kinds of narrative structure

We tell many different kinds of stories in various situations, whether we're gossiping with friends about what happened at the weekend, telling a joke, reading a bedtime story or writing a report of a scientific experiment. However, when we start to look for the structure of stories, some common patterns begin to emerge.

### Narrative structure 1: 'Cinderella'

Traditional fairy tales and nursery rhymes often illustrate some of the most common story narrative structures. Let's first look at 'Cinderella', an example of a very common four-part story structure:

| Structural element | Example |
|---|---|
| *Situation*: we are first given a situation that includes an element of instability | Cinderella is unhappy; she wants to go to the ball |
| *Complication*: then there is a development that complicates the situation in some way and introduces movement or change | The fairy godmother appears; Cinderella goes to the ball and meets the Prince |
| *Crisis*: eventually, the story reaches a crisis with a significant problem or conflict | Cinderella is whisked away at midnight, leaving one of her shoes behind. Will she ever see the Prince again? |
| *Resolution*: the problem is solved, and the situation is restored to one of stability | The shoes match; Cinderella marries her prince, and lives happily ever after . . . |

 See Module 3: Original Writing, The structure of fairy tales (page 116)

This structure allows many possible ways of creating interest, suspense, excitement and surprise, as we must wait for the resolution until the very end of the story.

### Narrative structure 2: Goldilocks visits the Three Bears

'Goldilocks and the Three Bears' is an example of another very common narrative structure in which the events of the story are organised into groups of three. This is sometimes referred to as a **triadic** structure:

| Goldilocks tries the chairs | Goldilocks tries the porridge | Goldilocks tries the beds |
|---|---|---|
| 1 Too big | 1 Too hot/salty | 1 Too hard |
| 2 Too small | 2 Too cold/sweet | 3 Too soft |
| 3 Just right | 3 Just right | 3 Just right |

When the bears return, the same triadic structure is repeated. In this structure, the third part is, of course, always the one that is conclusive – or in the case of three-part jokes, the one that delivers the punch line.

### Narrative structure 3: news reports

News stories, as reported in newspapers or bulletins, provide our third kind of structure. Here is a typical example drawn from a tabloid newspaper, the *Daily Mirror* (25 October 1999):

| Example | Structural element |
|---|---|
| **BRIGHT IDEA FOR XMAS** | *Headline provides a three or four word summary of the whole story* |
| Students have designed a genetically modified Christmas tree which could spell the end for traditional fairy lights. | *Starts with the whole story in a nutshell: who, what, why, when (not in this example), where (not in this example)* |
| Their Douglas Spruce has glow-in-the-dark pine needles produced by fluorescents found in jellyfish and fireflies. . . . The Hertfordshire University scholars calculate the tree would cost £200. | *Subsequent paragraphs simply add detail to any of these elements* |
| Student Katy Presland, 29, said: 'I'm sure a lot of people would love them, especially Americans.' | *May end with a quotation or comment relating to the whole story* |

There is no suspense involved with this structure: we discover the 'end' of the story right at the start. In fact, if space is short an editor can easily cut subsequent paragraphs without us losing the point of the story.

### Narrative structure 4: the 'whodunit'

Our fourth type of narrative structure is most clearly illustrated by detective fiction. Take this opening paragraph from Ruth Rendell's *The Veiled One*, one of her series of novels featuring Inspector Wexford:

> The woman was lying dead on the floor when he came in. She was already dead and covered up from head to toe but Wexford only knew that afterwards, not at the time. He looked back and realised the chances he had missed but it was useless doing that – he hadn't known and that was all.

As with news reports, we discover the event that represents the 'end' of the story right at the start. However, fans of Ruth Rendell's detective stories would be dismayed if the story had simply continued, as the news story structure might:

The dead woman, Elizabeth Smith, 28, had been shot in a revenge killing by Michael Jones, a former lover.

On the contrary, in detective fiction, we expect the rest of the story to consist of clues and flashbacks that will eventually enable us to reconstruct the events leading up to the death, and thus guess 'whodunit'.

## ACTIVITY 10

Think about the examples of narratives suggested in the table. For each of them decide which, if any, of our four structures best describes their organisation. If none seems to fit, try to define what their structure actually is.

**Narrative structures**

| Example of narrative | Discourse structure |
|---|---|
| Jokes: (1) There was an Englishman, Irishman and Scotsman . . . (2) [Supply one of your own] | |
| Personal anecdote: you tell your friends about something that happened to you at the weekend | |
| Excuse provided to teacher about non-completion of homework (Do you give the ending – 'I haven't done it' – at the start, or do you make it your punch line?!) | |
| A fairy story or nursery rhyme | |
| A typical episode of EastEnders | |

## Other discourse structures: written texts

Not all texts consist of stories. Some of the more common alternative discourse structures include *random lists*, such as shopping lists or things-to-do lists, and *sequenced lists/steps*, which are the result of more careful deliberation and may contain sets of instructions and explanations.

*Logical explanations/arguments* are likely to include explanations and solutions to problems, as well as persuasive arguments that may lead to a conclusion. These texts may start from an agreed or recognised fact, develop a series of logical steps arising from this fact, and then finish with a conclusion or question.

## ACTIVITY 11

Collect your own examples of written texts that appear to illustrate any three of the different discourse structures we've encountered so far.

### Discourse structure in speech: phone call (business)

How we use spoken language in familiar everyday situations is also structured in particular ways, though we may not be aware of it at the time. For example, many phone calls may follow a similar pattern to the one analysed in the table:

| Example | Structural element |
|---|---|
| A: 324667.<br>B: Oh hello. Is that Mr Jim Harrison?<br>A: Yeah, speaking.<br>B: This is Hayley Jones – you may remember we met some time ago.<br>A: Yes, of course. | *Exchange of identification of parties* |
| B: How are you? I hope I'm not calling at an inconvenient time.<br>A: No, no, not all. I'm fine. How are you?<br>B: Oh, pretty good. I'll tell you why I'm calling. It's about those books you ordered a while ago. | *Small talk, leading to identification of purpose of call* |
| B: We were just wondering if you'd received our invoice for the goods, and when we might expect to receive your payment?<br>A: Ah yes. I have it in front of me, actually. Thanks for that. You should be receiving our cheque over the next couple of days. | *Main business of call* |
| B: Oh that's good, Mr Harrison. We'll look forward to hearing from you then. Thanks for your help.<br>A: Not at all. If you'll excuse me, I've got someone waiting on the other line. | *Winding up, perhaps including a summary of what has been said, and a reason to close the conversation* |
| B: Of course. Goodbye now.<br>A: Bye. Talk to you soon. | *Exchange of goodbyes* |

## ACTIVITY 12

For each of the following speech situations, describe the stages the conversation is likely to go through – in other words, its typical discourse structure. Keep asking how such discourse typically begins, develops and concludes.

- making a confession/admission

- asking for a favour

- a doctor's appointment

- chatting someone up

## 2 Discourse layout, form and graphology

At the level of discourse structure, we are concerned with the inner construction of discourse in different contexts. At the level of form, we are interested in those features that contribute to the shape and (in writing) appearance of a text.

This is easier to discuss in terms of written texts, where the following questions all contribute to the total impact on the page:

- Is it arranged in columns, paragraphs, blocks or continuous text?

- Does it feature diagrams, pictures or other visual elements that connect to the text itself?

- What typefaces, type sizes and type styles (such as italic, bold) does it use?

Such features are collectively referred to as the **graphology** of a text.

## ACTIVITY 13

Find a typical example of each of the following texts, and then answer the questions above to define their graphological features.

- message in a greetings card

- tabloid newspaper report

- formal business letter from a company

- informative leaflet for the general public

- magazine aimed at an early teens readership

Now consider the following versions of the same summons to appear at a magistrates' court to answer a criminal charge. What different 'messages' are being conveyed by the different typefaces? Which are the most and least appropriate typefaces?

*1 Typeface: Playbill*

You are hereby summoned to appear at Newtown Magistrates' Court on Tuesday, February 13th at 10.30 am to answer charges that on November 14th, 1998, you did wilfully commit an act of disorderly conduct.

*2 Typeface: Braggadocio*

**You are hereby summoned to appear at Newtown Magistrates' Court on Tuesday, February 13th at 10.30 am to answer charges that on November 14th, 1998, you did wilfully commit an act of disorderly conduct.**

*3 Typeface: Brush Script MT*

*You are hereby summoned to appear at Newtown Magistrates' Court on Tuesday, February 13th at 10.30 am to answer charges that on November 14th, 1998, you did wilfully commit an act of disorderly conduct.*

*4 Typeface: Desdemona*

YOU ARE HEREBY SUMMONED TO APPEAR AT NEWTOWN MAGISTRATES' COURT ON TUESDAY, FEBRUARY 13TH AT 10.30 AM TO ANSWER CHARGES THAT ON NOVEMBER 14TH, 1998, YOU DID WILFULLY COMMIT AN ACT OF DISORDERLY CONDUCT.

The 'forms' of spoken discourse may be less obvious, but if we ask some basic questions about different kinds of conversation we can begin to describe the typical 'shapes' that they usually take.

## ACTIVITY 14

Complete the missing sections in the table to describe the forms of these common discourse types:

| Question | Job interview | Classroom lesson | Live football commentary | Formal meeting |
|---|---|---|---|---|
| Who takes part? | One or more employers and an interviewee | | Main commentator and an 'expert' adviser | |
| What are the usual circumstances and context? | An office or other room on business premises | A classroom in a school or college | | A committee room or similar, with members sitting round a desk/table |
| What are the roles of the speakers? What kinds of thing do they say? | | Teacher leads, asking questions, evaluating answers, giving instructions and explanations, and maintaining discipline | | Chair manages the meeting, taking it through the agenda, and maintains orderly discussion |

## 3 Sentences: length, construction and function

At sentence level we begin to look at those aspects of language that people think of when they use the word grammar. In fact, grammar can include a description of how language works at any of our five levels. The term **syntax** is used when discussing the ways sentences are put together by placing words in a particular order.

### Length

However, perhaps the first and easiest way of distinguishing how sentences are used in a particular text is to comment on their length. Some texts may use predominantly short sentences – like this children's story, *Floppy the Hero*, by Roderick Hunt:

A fire engine went by. There was a fire. Everyone ran to see. 'Get back,' said a fireman. A barn was on fire.

It is not only writers for children who deliberately keep their sentences short. Sometimes writing in this way can convey tension or excitement, as in this extract from the novel *Things Fall Apart*, in which Nigerian writer Chinua Achebe captures the atmosphere of a tribal wrestling match:

At last the two teams danced into the circle and the crowd roared and clapped. The drums rose to a frenzy. The people surged forwards. The young men who kept order flew around, waving their palm fronds.

### Construction

Very short sentences are also, by definition, simply constructed. For this reason it is easy to confuse length and complexity. In fact, even longer sentences can still be relatively simple. Consider these two sentences, of identical length (48 words):

A  It was a nice canny game an all but sometimes windows used to get brocken and another thing in them days people were lucky if they had indoor netties and it was bloody murder if you wanted to gan to the toilet in the middle of the neet.

B  Not having had prior knowledge of the events which were about to unfold, and being possessed of the mistaken assumption that his way in the world was to be one of unimpeded progress, Michael was ill prepared for the news with which he would be greeted that morning.

Although of identical length, the sentence in Extract A strikes us as simpler than that in Extract B because of the ways in which it joins together its various parts (mainly using 'and' and 'but' to string them together). Extract B, in contrast, uses more grammatically complex ways of linking the sentence elements together ( 'not having had', 'with which he would be'. . .).

The stylistics framework also reminds us to ask whether a text is written using complete, 'correct' sentences, and whether it uses any examples of unusual word order. Our usual notion of what constitutes a 'complete' sentence is based on written language; in speech, utterances like 'Hi Alan' and 'It is', which are technically not 'complete sentences', are very common. Some written texts also use an abbreviated or note form in the interests of economy.

As for word order, we may often find unusual examples in poems. Look back at pages 6 and 7, and in particular Extract D, 'The Passionate Shepherd to his Love' ('we will all the pleasures prove' rather than 'we will prove all the pleasures'), and Extract G, 'The Jumblies' ('In a Sieve they went to sea' following the more usual 'They went to sea in a Sieve'). Writers – and speakers too – may choose to play around with word order for many reasons.

## Function

 We shall investigate sentence structures and syntax in more detail in *A2 English Language*: Module 3. Investigation.

Another relatively simple way of describing the kinds of sentences used in any piece of discourse is to ask what job or function they are most commonly carrying out. Here is one framework that identifies four sentence functions:

- The most common sentence type is the statement or declarative. This can be a statement of fact, an event, a feeling, an opinion or a prediction.

- Another type of sentence is the question or interrogative

- A third type is the direct command, or imperative

- The exclamation is a rarer type of sentence. Exclamations can include very short utterances like 'Great goal!'

## ACTIVITY 15

Go back to the nine texts we looked at earlier (see pages 6–8). For any of these, count the instances of each sentence type occurring in the extract, then use a pie chart or bar chart to record your findings. Compare your results with the commentary on page 48.

For example, Extract A (the teacher's instructions) might look something like this:

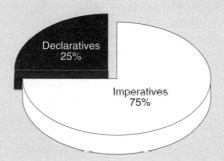

Declaratives 25%

Imperatives 75%

For any of the following types of text, try to predict the proportions in which you will find the four kinds of sentence:

- a manual for a piece of computer software

- an editorial 'leader' or similar comment column in a newspaper

- an interview with a celebrity in a magazine

Now find some examples of these kinds of text and count the numbers of each sentence type to test your prediction.

Finally, try to explain why the texts should have more of one type of sentence than another. Think about the purpose and subject matter of the texts themselves.

## 4 Words and phrases

The vocabulary of a language is known as its **lexis**. As the number of questions included in the stylistics framework (see pages 11–13) suggests, at this level there is always a lot to observe.

It is useful here to be able to describe accurately different kinds of words and the jobs they do in a sentence, as well as their meanings. Word classes provide one traditional framework for doing this.

Let's look again at Extract C on page 6, the eye-witness testimony from the Titanic. The following words from the extract have something in common:

We (×2) ship Wednesday morning April drill Cherbourg Queenstown Sunday (×3) it afternoon night I watch noise cable ship anchor shock

All of these words are involved in various kinds of naming. As such, they all belong to the word class of nouns. We can subdivide this class like this:

| Word class description | Function | Examples |
|---|---|---|
| proper nouns | names of specific places, months, days, people | Cherbourg, Queenstown, April, Sunday |
| concrete nouns | names of objects | ship, cable, anchor |
| abstract nouns | names of feelings or ideas | shock |
| pronouns | substitutes for names of people and things | we, it |

Similarly, let's look now at these words from Extract E (Windows installation, page 6):

> upgrade Insert click (×3) Type Note install precede Follow continue

These are words that describe actions, so they belong to the class of verbs. Not all verbs describe actions; others describe feelings ('I hate you!') or existence ('I am', 'you are' 's/he is', etc.).

Now consider the function of these words from Extract I, *Sons and Lovers* (page 8):

> dry wet nasty

They all add descriptive information about the noun to which they refer. So Morel's singlet (a concrete noun) is variously referred to as dry, wet and nasty. This places these words in the class of adjectives, which qualify or provide additional information about a noun.

Now look at the word 'gingerly' from the same passage. This is also descriptive, but it describes not the singlet itself but the action of feeling it. It therefore belongs to the class of adverbs, which provide information about a verb (usually how, where or when it occurs).

These major word classes are the ones likely to be most useful in stylistic 'finger-printing'. They are listed along with prepositions and conjunctions in the table.

## Principal word classes

| Word class | Function | Subclasses | Examples |
|---|---|---|---|
| nouns | Name specific people, places, times; things; feelings, ideas | proper; concrete; abstract | London, Tony Blair, Christmas; jelly, rocks, anorak; happiness, equality |
| pronouns | Substitute for or refer to nouns | (im)personal; possessive | (it) I, me, you, s/he, we, they; my, mine, your, his, hers, its, yours, theirs |
| adjectives | Provide additional information about nouns | factual; opinionative | blue, steel, six; awful, excellent |
| adverbs | Provide additional information about verbs | manner (= how); time (= when); place (= where) | quickly, unpleasantly; then, now; here, everywhere |
| conjunctions | Join phrases together within a sentence | co-ordinating; subordinating (these terms are explored in English Language A2) | and, but, so; because, although, despite |
| prepositions | Define positions and relationships | | in, on, between, against, over, under |

## ACTIVITY 16

Look back at some of the short texts you collected for Activity 2 on page 4. For any of these texts, identify and highlight examples of each principal word class. Make a list of these items on separate pieces of paper – one each for nouns, verbs, adjectives, adverbs, conjunctions and prepositions – in the order in which they appear in the text.

Give the lists one at a time to a partner, and for each one invite them to predict the nature of the text on the basis of the listed words. At the end, discuss which word class enabled your partner(s) to identify the type of text most easily, and why this might be.

## Using word classes within the stylistics framework

If we return to the key questions, we can now use word classes systematically as a means of investigating some important aspects of 'linguistic fingerprints'.

## ACTIVITY 17

Look again at Extract H on page 8, the address by John Ball. Your task is to write a detailed analysis of the way the speech uses language to inspire its audience.

Start with an overview of the text in which you explain its purpose and context. Then work through the word class questions as suggested in the table. Finally, compare your results with the commentary on page 49.

| Key question | Word class investigation |
|---|---|
| How much of the text conveys facts and how much conveys opinions? Is the language emotional or detached? | (1) The most obvious words to look at are the adjectives and adverbs. Ask whether they convey factual or emotional or opinionative details about the noun or verb they describe. (2) However, nouns and verbs can be just as revealing. Compare, for example: (i) 'The soldier moved away' (ii) 'The deserter fled' and (iii) 'The hero retreated'. |
| Does the text seem personal or impersonal? | We can usually answer this question by looking at the pronouns. There are three aspects to consider: (1) Does the writer or speaker draw attention to him/herself by using 'I' (the first person singular)? (2) Does s/he use the first person plural ('we', 'our'), and if so, who does it include or refer to? (3) Does the speaker/writer use 'you' (the second person) to address readers or listeners directly? |
| | If the answer to all three of these questions is 'no', then we can safely describe the language as impersonal. |

| | |
|---|---|
| Is the text formal/neutral/informal? Is it simple or sophisticated? Does it include words that belong to a particular subject or theme, or that are specialist, technical, literary or old-fashioned? | Here we are considering the register of a text. Nouns and verbs are likely to be central, but consider adjectives and adverbs too. Even conjunctions and prepositions (such as 'therefore', 'hitherto') can help mark out a text as rather formal. |
| Are there any non-standard or regional expressions? | This is a matter of the dialect of a text. Most written English is in Standard English, though some writers (like D. H. Lawrence in Extract I, from *Sons and Lovers*) may try to capture regional speech on paper. Spoken discourse is much more likely to include dialectal variations, which may use alternative nouns and verbs for everyday items and actions. And there may be other differences from Standard English – such as unusual plurals ('childer' for children, etc.) or different present and past tenses (such as 'I were', 'you was'). See the section 'Accents and dialects' later in this module (page 36). |
| Is language being used in its literal sense – or does it use similes and/or metaphors and other figurative expressions? | Although single words may be metaphorical – 'You're such an angel! (noun), or 'I've got to scoot!' (verb), for example – we often need to consider whole phrases here. English makes deliberate use of similes, metaphors and other expressions to convey meanings more vividly, but bear in mind that the language also contains many everyday words and phrases that are idiomatic (their meanings cannot be guessed from their literal sense). |

## ACTIVITY 18

It is not just poets and writers of English literature who use similes and metaphors. On the contrary, ordinary everyday speech is full of expressions, or idioms, which are not intended to be taken literally. Some of the most common to be heard at the moment include: 'at the end of the day', 'the bottom line is . . .', 'a level playing field', and 'moving the goalposts'.

Collect additional examples of other such phrases in common use – and note down their probable origin. For example, 'a level playing field' and 'moving the goalposts' are clearly drawn from football.

Many common expressions in everyday use are based on metaphors, but they are so familiar that we take them for granted. List – and look out for – examples of these two:

- where 'high' is good and 'down' is bad – such as 'I'm on cloud nine', 'She's down in the dumps'.

- where life is a journey – such as 'You're on the right track', 'He's gone off the rails', 'What's the next step?'

## 5 Sounds and spellings

The relationship between the sounds of spoken English and the way we spell our words is the subject of the later section on speaking and writing. However, even on the evidence of the nine texts at the start of this module, it is clear that some written texts include unusual spellings. In the case of Extract I from *Sons and Lovers*, D. H. Lawrence uses non-standard spellings in an attempt to suggest Morel's regional accent:

An' iv'ry day alike my singlet's wringin' wet.

Historical texts may also surprise us with unfamiliar spellings of familiar words that reflect changes in language over time. And a flick through your local Yellow Pages can reveal how advertisers such as Kwik-Fit deliberately alter spellings to grab our attention – also a favourite technique among pop and rock bands.

## ACTIVITY 19

For each of the categories in the table, collect six additional examples of variant spellings. Try to suggest exactly how the alternative spelling affects the way you respond to the name of the company or group.

| Cafés and restaurants | Card shops | Groups and bands |
|---|---|---|
| The Koffee Kup<br>Brewers' Fayre<br>Donut Magik | Cards 'r' Us<br>Kelly's Kards<br>Wishing U Well | The Beatles<br>Boyzone |

The aspect of language study concerned with sounds is called **phonology**, which we consider in some detail in the section on speaking and writing (see page 30 below). We can sometimes observe noticeable patterns in the way particular sounds are used in written texts. These include:

- rhythm

- rhyme

- alliteration (Peter Piper picked a peck of pickled pepper)

- onomatopoeia (pop, sizzle, splash)

Of these, perhaps the most difficult to write about is rhythm. We can see how rhythm works at its simplest by looking again at Extract G (page 8), 'The Jumblies'. Musicians are used to talking about the beats in a passage of music; similarly, with verse we can usually feel where the natural 'beat' of the language falls.

## ACTIVITY 20

Work through the activities suggested alongside 'The Jumblies' in the table.

| Text | Activity/commentary |
|------|---------------------|
| They **went** to **sea** in a **Sieve**, they **did**, <br> In a **Sieve** they **went** to **sea**: <br> In **spite** of **all** their **friends** could **say**, <br> On a **win**ter's **morn**, on a **stor**my **day**, <br> In a **Sieve** they **went** to **sea**! | (1) Read these lines aloud and note how the 'beat' falls on the syllables in bold. These beats are usually referred to as stresses in verse. What sort of pattern begins to emerge? (2) You'll see that there seems to be a pattern of 4–3–4–4–3 **stresses** in each line, but that the 'three-beat' lines seem to have an invisible pause built in. Just as in music, where silent beats are marked with a rest, in rhythmical verse the pauses are built in to the rhythm. |

## ACTIVITY 21

Gather some samples of the types of texts shown in the table. Identify the specific linguistic sound effects used and write them in the second column. In each case, try to explain how the effect makes the text achieve its purpose for the intended audience.

| Data/texts | Sound effects used (alliteration, assonance, rhyme, rhythm, onomatopoeia, etc.) |
|---|---|
| Advertising slogans/jingles | |
| Children's verse | |
| Tabloid news headlines | |

## ACTIVITY 22

C3.3

It's time to put the whole of our stylistics framework into practice. We'll use a single text, an advertisement for a product called CDfender which appeared in *Q* magazine, a music periodical with a readership in the 20–35 age group, in September/October 1999.

The basic question is, as always: how does this text use language to achieve its purpose for the intended audience? A good analysis requires a systematic approach to the task.

An approach:

*1 First reading:* during your first reading of the text, try to answer these basic questions, jotting down your responses in rough:

- What is the text saying to its audience?

- Who are its audience?

- What is the text doing to its audience?

- What, in general terms, do you think is the intended impact of the text on its audience?

# CURRY ON THE HOUSE

Or it could be fag ash on Ash. Or beer all over your best Cardigans. Basically, CDs come to more sticky ends than Kenny.

And try to play a damaged CD and it just st-st-st-st-sticks and j    umps.

So how do you stop your favourite hip hop hopping all over the place?

Or your Garbage sounding rubbish?

With CDfender.

It's an optical quality polycarbonate film that keeps CDs as squeaky clean as The Corrs.

Just peel off the backing and press CDfender on the disc. It can stay put

longer than a crusty's socks, the laser reading through it as if it wasn't there.

CDfender works on games CDs and CD-ROMs too.

House or garage, jungle or country, it's the ultimate cover.

| Questions | Responses |
| --- | --- |
| What is the text saying to its audience? | They risk damaging their precious CDs unless they use CDfender to protect them. It does so very well. |
| Who are its audience? | *Q* readers; music fans. |
| What is the text doing to its audience? | Amusing them with its wit while persuading them to buy the product. |
| What, in general terms, do you think is the intended impact of the text on its audience? | They may quite enjoy the nature of the jokes and recognise a problem that they have experienced themselves, tempting them to consider the usefulness of CDfender. |

### Sample first response

*2 Second/third/fourth readings:* now ask the big 'How?' question – how is language used to achieve all of this? Make pencil jottings in rough as you re-read it several times, noting the most striking aspects of the language and their impact.

*3 Apply the framework:* before starting to write up your analysis, use the five-level stylistic framework, with its different kinds of questions at each level, as a checklist. Have you found something to say about: structure; form/graphology; sentences; lexis (vocabulary and phrases); sounds and spelling?

*4 Writing your analysis:* now write up your analysis. You can comment on the text bit by bit as you go along, but it may be better to use the framework as a way of organising your analysis into five sections.

Either way, it's good to start with a brief summary of your answers to the 'What?' questions. Remember: you need to relate all your observations about how the language is being used to its context (that is, its purpose, medium and audience).

Now compare your analysis with the commentary on this text on page 50.

## Speaking and writing

An understanding of the relationship between spoken and written language is central to much of the work you will do on the course as a whole, and is also a key element of this module. Here are some of the questions we need to ask about speech and writing:

- Is writing just speech written down?

- Is writing more 'grammatical' than speech?

- When is it better to use one rather than the other?

To start to answer these questions, let's look at a pair of parallel pieces of data. The first is a transcript of an oral account given by a witness to an accident, and the second the written statement she subsequently produced.

| Speech (transcript) | Writing (statement) |
| --- | --- |
| A: Did you see what happened?<br>B: Well – er – not really – er – I was just walking the dog like – you know – it was not long turned dark – and we'd been down the alley there and back – and – er – then this car comes racing down here – so – as I turned round there was this bloody great crash – you know – screeching tyres and everything – so I turn round and there's black smoke pouring out where it had crashed like.<br><br>A: Could you see if anyone was hurt?<br>B: Well – I was standing over there – at the far end of those shops – and – and – like I say it were dark and there was all the smoke – and I just thought – some poor bugger has had it like – you know – | At approximately 8.30 last night I witnessed an accident involving a blue Ford Sierra on Abbey Road, Barrow.<br><br>I heard the sound of a car approaching, apparently at some speed, before it braked suddenly and subsequently crashed into the wall near the junction with Dalton Road. Black smoke immediately began to pour from the vehicle, and I assumed that the driver must have been seriously hurt. |

## ACTIVITY 23

Let's consider these two accounts from Activity 22 in more detail. Work through the following questions, then compare your responses with the commentary on page 52.

- Although the transcript includes the words – and some of the hesitations – in the witness's account, many aspects of her speech are still absent. What aspects are missing from the transcript, and what would they have contributed to the meanings she was trying to convey?

- Some elements of the spoken account are absent from the written statement. What are these, and why do you think they are missing?

- Look now at the ways in which sentences are formed in both versions. What differences do you notice?

- The spoken version includes some references to places (such as 'here', 'there') that are made more explicit in the written account. Why do you think this is?

- How does the witness's use of verbs differ in her two accounts?

- In general terms, what seems to be the difference between the style and register of the two versions, and what might account for this?

## Characteristics and functions of speaking and writing

The differences between spoken and written language that we are beginning to explore have implications for the ways in which we may choose to use them in a range of situations. We'll start to look at some of these in the following activity.

---

**ACTIVITY 24**                                                    C3.1A

Consider the sets of contrasts between speaking and writing presented in the table, and discuss the questions raised in the second column:

| Differences between speaking and writing | Questions |
| --- | --- |
| Much of what is communicated in speech comes from paralinguistic and prosodic features, whereas writing depends entirely on the words on a page. | Which is most likely to reveal dishonesty or insincerity? Which would you prefer to use if you needed to deceive someone? |
| Speech is unplanned, and may include slips and mistakes of all kinds. Writing can be re-drafted: mistakes can be removed before it is seen. | When might it be desirable to use writing to avoid making unplanned slips? |
| Speech is momentary, unless taped, whereas writing offers a permanent record. | When might you need to keep a record of a communication? |
| As listeners, we have no control over the speed of the delivery and may have to interrupt to ask for information to be repeated or clarified. As readers, we can stop and re-read at our own pace. | What are the advantages and disadvantages of (1) listening to a presentation and (2) reading a book as a means of gaining information? |

---

## Sounds and spelling

We can investigate further the relationship between spoken and written language by considering the sounds that make up the words we use, and the letters with which we represent them on paper.

In English, we usually categorise these sounds as either vowels or consonants. Collectively, these sounds – the building bricks from which everything in our language is ultimately constructed – are called **phonemes**.

## ACTIVITY 25

Take one of our common vowel phonemes – the sound represented by the letters 'ee' as used in 'feet'. Find examples of other words that contain the same phoneme but represent it using a different spelling. You should be able to find at least four different ones!

Compare your findings with the commentary on page 52.

By using pairs of letters as well as single ones to represent phonemes, we make the 26 letters of the alphabet capable of expressing more than 26 sounds. Other examples are the sounds represented by '*sh-*' and '*ch-*', though in both cases there is still no single way of representing them – think of 'ship' and 'station', 'church' and 'cello'. Some other phonemes in English do correspond more closely with the written alphabet: the letter 'd', for instance, does usually express the sound *d* – though even here the letter may be used on its own ('dog') or in a pair ('ladder') to represent the same sound.

Another oddity is that the most common vowel sound in English does not have a letter associated with it, and is expressed using a huge variety of spelling combinations. Say aloud the vowel sound represented by the letters in bold in each of the words below:

*banana undeniable natural rubber custard*
In each case, depending on your regional accent, you will probably be making a short rather abrupt sound something like 'uh'. This surprising little vowel is, in fact, the phoneme linguists call schwa. In total, there are 44 phonemes in most accents of English.

## Speech in conversation: analysing talk

Mostly, however, we are entirely unconscious of the individual phonemes we are combining when we engage in the most common of linguistic activities – talk. The most interesting thing about talk is how we interact as social beings. We use language not just to exchange information but also to negotiate our social relationships.

We have already explored ways in which the structures of certain conversational situations typically follow a recognisable pattern. For instance, an encounter with friends may start with a greeting and some small talk, move to anecdotes about what you've each been doing, and end with excuses for leave-taking ('Well, must  be going . . .', etc.) followed by repeated 'bye', 'see you', 'take care', 'be in touch', or other similar phrases (see page 17).

So what are the factors that determine the form of a particular kind of talk, or the sorts of things people say in a particular situation?

## ACTIVITY 26

In groups, discuss how each of the following factors might influence the part you play in a conversation, and the vocabulary, expressions, tone of voice and accent you use:

- the place where a conversation occurs (at home, in class, at a party, in church, at the workplace . . .)

- who else is present (friends, family, teachers, workmates, boss . . .)

- the purpose of the conversation (social chat, job interview, buying/selling, asking a favour . . .)

Now compare your responses with the commentary on page 53.

## A framework for analysing talk

Earlier, we applied a systematic method to the stylistic analysis of a written text (see pages 11–12). Now let's try something similar for speech, but starting from a different set of questions:

### A framework for analysing talk

| Key question | Explanation |
|---|---|
| Who seems to lead the talk? | This means looking closely at how the talk moves on as each speaker takes their turn. These alternating turns are referred to as **adjacency pairs**. In some situations, the pattern may be obvious – a teacher or a police officer may ask all the questions, for instance. |
| Who says what gets talked about? | The ability to influence the subject or 'agenda' of a conversation is usually a sign of personal status or dominance. In formal talk, the agenda and who controls it (or **topic management**, as this aspect of talk is known) may be obvious; in informal situations, where many topics may be covered, we need to look more closely at whose subjects get talked about and whose don't. |
| Who talks most? | Always a key question, but the answer to this question will not always lead us to the dominant speaker. Sometimes, the most powerful person needs to say very little. |
| Who interrupts? Who backs down? | This is usually an interesting question. If someone is easily interrupted this may be a sign of low status, whereas the right to speak uninterrupted is often an indicator of conversational dominance. |

| Who gets to comment on what people say? | In classrooms, teachers routinely say in response to students 'Good answer', 'Well done', or 'That's right' (or their opposites). However, when a teacher asks a particularly searching question, students seldom say 'Good question, sir'. The right to make judgements about what other people say is often a sign of status or power. |
|---|---|
| What are people trying to do to other speakers? . . . Or, what do people really mean? | When we start to talk about the weather, is it always because we are obsessed with meteorology, or is it simply a way of saying to each other 'Let's talk. Let's be friendly'? The study of what we really mean and intend with our speech is called pragmatics. |

## A C T I V I T Y   2 7

To put this into practice, we'll look closely at the piece of spontaneous speech we saw earlier in Extract F (page 7). It was recorded from a late night Radio Phone-in.

Re-read the transcript below with this basic question in mind: what do you notice about the way this conversation works and the language used by each speaker? Re-read the data, making sure you apply the questions in our framework.

A: Tanya from West Shields on line 2. Hi Tanya.
T: Hi Alan.
A: Helloa, the best and the worst from you.
T: The best for me was going to Canada – em – 4 years ago to see an adopted sister.
A: Right – which –
T: I'd never met before.
A: Which lump of Canada was it?
T: Er, Toronto and then I flew on to Winnipeg.
A: Oh great. I mean what's – you always get the impression that Canada's – like – just massive, this immense country. What –
T: It is.
A: What's it actually like?

Compare your notes with those made by a student, reprinted in the commentary on page 52. The student has offered some interesting comments on the data.

Then try to list the specific questions that the student's comments seem to answer. Try to phrase the questions so that they could apply to any piece of conversation – for example, 'How do the speakers address each other?'.

 We return to more analysis of talk and pragmatics in Module 2, Language and Social Contexts (see page 57).

# You and your language: idiolect, dialect and sociolect

So far, we have focused mainly on the ways in which language varies according to the context, audience, purpose and medium in which it is used. We have talked about what we described as the individual linguistic fingerprints of texts, and begun to learn how to recognise and describe these. One of our initial language queries went further, and also raised the possibility of such 'fingerprints' for individual speakers; indeed, our everyday experience suggests that individuals often have distinctive ways of using language.

In this section we explore this notion, and the kinds of influences that help to determine our individual linguistic identities.

## Your language history and experience

### ACTIVITY 28

For each of the possible sources of influence shown in the table, try to suggest the ways in which they affected your personal language development. As you consider each one, think about how it might have influenced:

- the role you tend to play in conversations

- your accent

- your grammar

- your choice of words, phrases and slang

| Source of influence | Nature and strength of influence |
| --- | --- |
| Parents | |
| Brothers and sisters | |
| The places where you lived | |
| Teachers | |
| Books | |
| Groups of friends | |
| TV, music and other media | |
| Places you have worked | |

Compare your own experiences with those of other members of the group, and then compare your group's response with the commentary on page 54.

## Defining your individuality: idiolect

In Activity 28, we saw that the way in which each individual speaker uses language is the result of a complex interaction of influences and circumstances. Perhaps the spider diagram helps to simplify the picture:

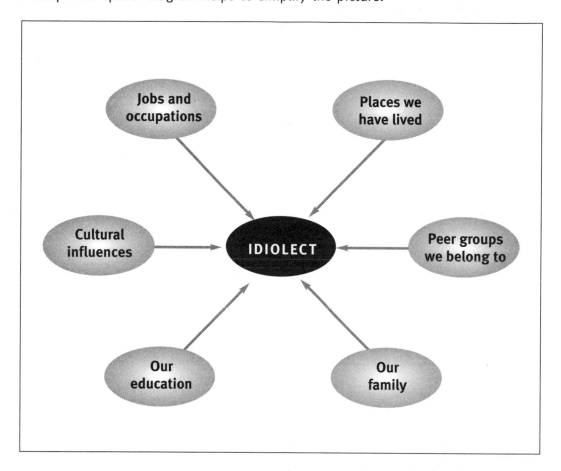

All the distinguishing features that together contribute to your own unique use of language comprise your idiolect.

### ACTIVITY 29

Your task is to define for a friend or partner exactly what makes his or her speech unique. Working with your partner, consider in turn each of the aspects of speech listed in the table on the next page, and try to arrive at a detailed profile for each other's distinctive speech.

Compile profiles for each other, and then share the results with other pairs. It may help to start by taping each other in a reasonably natural speaking situation; then work with the recordings as you try to complete the profiles.

## Idiolect: your language profile

| Feature | Questions to ask | Your partner's characteristics |
|---|---|---|
| Pitch | How high, or low, is the voice in most contexts? | |
| Tempo | Is the speaker's speed of delivery average, or slower or faster than average? | |
| Timbre (quality of voice) | Does the voice sound 'rough', 'hard' or 'soft'? 'Bright' or 'husky'? | |
| Intonation | Does the voice go up and down a lot as s/he speaks, or does it stay closer to a flat monotone? | |
| Accent | How strong a regional accent does s/he speak with? How close to RP? | |
| Dialect | Does s/he use any regional words or constructions? | |
| Fillers | Does s/he tend to use non-verbal fillers (e.g. 'er', 'um'), or does s/he have a favourite verbal filler (e.g. 'you know what I mean', 'sort of hair')? | |
| Words and phrases | Does s/he favour words from a particular register, or use particular examples of slang or swearing? | |

## Accents and dialects

The extracts we considered at the start of this module included some examples of English that were clearly different from the 'standard' version we usually encounter in print. For example, in D. H. Lawrence's *Sons and Lovers* (Extract I on page 8), the speech of Mr Morel is represented in such a way as to suggest his broad Nottinghamshire accent and dialect. This is, of course, a piece of fiction. But what are Britain's regional varieties really like?

Let's begin by looking at a transcript of a Sunderland man, aged 60, reminiscing about life when he was a child. Some attempt has been made to reflect the more interesting pronunciations using non-standard spellings.

When I was a bairn – many years ago – does tha want to know – grandma – that's mi mother – used to play bloody waar – when we used to come in on a night – and we'd all been plodgin – down in the bourn – that's a stream which is down near the beck – all our clathes were up the eyes in clarts – and mi ma used to say – you cannot ave any more money for any more ket this week – so – me and mi mates used to gan and clean pigeon crees out for the men who used to fly pigeons – when they come back they used to hoy them mebbies down in Bradford – they used to flee back – and we used to clean the cree out and he used to give us some money – to buy our own ket . . . What else does tha want to know? – tha disn'y know when you're weel off you people – does tha want to know what we used to do for holidays – we used to gerron a bus – and gan down to Seaborne about 7 mile away – nae Blackpools – nae Majorcas – nae bloody Ibizas – or bloody Tenerifes – we never had nowt like that – never thout on.

## ACTIVITY 30

Discuss and write an analysis of the Sunderland man's speech in which you identify the ways in which this speaker's language differs from Standard English. Then compare your findings with the commentary on page 55.

You might find it helpful to distinguish between *pronunciation* (as far as you can tell from the spellings), *vocabulary* and *grammar*.

As you worked on Activity 30 you were beginning to make a distinction between two terms that are often confused. When focusing on the aspects of the speaker's pronunciation, you were looking at accent, whereas the vocabulary and grammar of a variety of language define which **dialect** it belongs to. We have already met the terms 'Received Pronunciation' and 'Standard English'; these refer to an accent and a dialect respectively, though they are both rather special because they enjoy the prestige of being regarded as 'correct', 'good' or 'proper' English and are not native to any one region.

Attitudes towards other accents and dialects vary considerably. Some accents – often those such as Glasgow and Birmingham, associated with large urban areas – prove consistently unpopular and unglamorous, whereas others – such as the rural accents of the south-west of England or East Anglian rural accents – are perceived as 'quaint'. A third group of regional accents is highly regarded because the accents seem to combine friendliness with intelligence, which makes them ideal for companies seeking staff for large call centres.

 This topic is covered in detail in Module 2, Language and Social Contexts.

Attitudes towards dialects are equally mixed: people are often intrigued and charmed by the non-standard words of our regions, and fearful that we may be losing many of them – as the *Observer* article in the next activity suggests.

## ACTIVITY 31

Read the article carefully. Make a note of the evidence and explanations it offers for the claim that dialect lexis is disappearing. What appears to be the writer's attitude to this development? What do you think will be lost if our dialectal vocabulary disappears?

# OUR DISAPPEARING DIALECTS

(THE *OBSERVER*, 31 OCTOBER 1999)

Britain's rich fund of slang is fast dwindling. Terms such as 'cow-pawed' or 'thwart-eyed' – insults meaning left-handed or cross-eyed which were once commonplace in their native communities – are not thought likely to make it far into the next century.

Many regional forms of invective are already extinct, and the trend is set to continue.

The English spoken in Britain appears to be shedding its quirks comparatively faster than languages spoken in surrounding Western countries.

The power of standard English seems to be a stronger force here than elsewhere', explained Leeds University lecturer Dr Clive Upton.

The decrease in the use of words such as 'urchin' for a hedgehog and 'lop' for a flea is the result of increased mobility in the population. In the past 50 years people's need to deal with others over a wider geographical area has put a premium on clear communication.

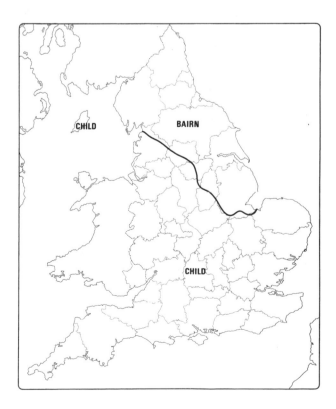

Dr Clive Upton, the researcher mentioned in the article, helped to compile a linguistic atlas of Britain and has produced maps that show the geographical distribution of hundreds of dialect terms (*Word Maps: A Dialect Atlas of England*). For example, if we return to our Sunderland speaker's use of 'bairn' and 'clarts', the maps indicate that 'bairn' is retreating northwards as the Standard English form 'child' becomes increasingly universal, and that 'clarts' is only one of many alternatives to the Standard English 'mud' spread throughout the country.

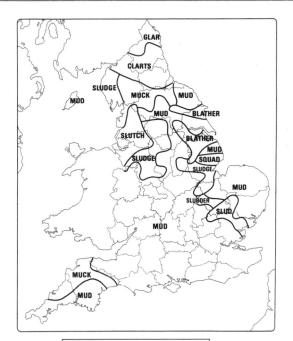

Many dialect words have a very long history, and survive as relics of different dialects first brought to Britain by various Anglo-Saxon and Viking invaders. The Lonely Planet series of travel books, which usually concentrates on information and phrases for British travellers overseas, has published a British phrasebook documenting examples of such regional differences.

## ACTIVITY 32

Check your region against these maps. Do you recognise the items quoted as belonging to your dialect? Or can you find other examples of your region's dialect?

Carry out interviews with members of your family or neighbours, especially more elderly ones, because if Upton is right younger speakers are no longer familiar with many dialect terms. It might be interesting to interview older people who were brought up in different parts of the country.

One useful approach is to ask your interviewees to suggest alternative words for terms that often show marked regional variations. Try: a narrow alleyway running between houses; a blister or blemish on the skin; a gooseberry; a silly or stupid person; and a splinter (of wood).

Although people remain interested in and sympathetic to regional lexis, attitudes towards the distinctive grammar of regional dialects are often more hostile. Consider the examples of dialect speech in the next activity, which are quoted from Peter Trudgill's *The Dialects of England* (1990).

## ACTIVITY 33

For each of these examples, decide whether or not you consider it to be 'good' grammar, and suggest a Standard English equivalent.

| Example | 'Good' grammar? | SE equivalent |
|---|---|---|
| them books there | | |
| she sings nice | | |
| I don't want no trouble | | |
| Are any of youse coming? | | |
| I never seed he | | |
| I sees the dentist tomorrow | | |
| He ain't coming | | |
| Give us a kiss | | |

Now compare your responses with the commentary on page 55.

## Fitting in: language as a membership card

As we saw earlier, an important influence on the ways we use language is the social group or network to which we belong. Of course, we all belong to many different groupings, so we develop different styles of language to suit the group we are with at any one time. All kinds of groupings – family, friends, workmates, football supporters, doctors, fans of a particular pop band – may develop distinctive uses of language that come to characterise them and indicate their identity to others.

As with many clubs, to join one of these groups may involve some sort of initiation process; we learn its rules, its passwords, its rituals and its traditions. Perhaps most important of all, we may have to learn the language of the group – in other words, acquire its **sociolect**.

## ACTIVITY 34

Start by listing the various social groups you belong to at different times. The table suggests some possibilities, but try to add some of your own.

Then ask yourself: what is distinctive about the ways in which this group uses language? (Remember to think at different levels of linguistic analysis.) The distinguishing features could be: certain rituals or patterns of interaction; particular constructions, or examples of non-standard grammar; a specialist vocabulary, or 'in' buzzwords or slang; a particular accent or style of pronunciation.

Record your suggestions in the table, then read the commentary on page 56.

| Social groups | Distinctive features of the group's language |
|---|---|
| Your family | |
| Your immediate group of friends | |
| People who live in your town or region | |
| People who share a particular interest | |
| People who do the same job | |
| People from the same social background | |
| People who like the same kind of music | |
| People who support the same team | |
| | |
| | |
| | |
| | |

## Inclusion and exclusion

In many ways, a sociolect can act as a membership badge which proclaims the fact that you belong to, and identify with, a particular social group. A sociolect is just like a whole language, but in miniature. If we go to live and work in a foreign country, to be fully accepted as a member of that community may well entail learning the native language, customs and traditions. On a smaller scale, 'outsiders' who wish to join and be accepted by social groups may need to learn and adopt language features that characterise the group in order to fit in. This could mean a slight change in their accent, using a particular kind of vocabulary, or observing certain linguistic rituals.

However, this can cut both ways. We may be members of a group that doesn't want outsiders to join us or to understand the meanings we are communicating to each other. In this case, the group may develop a sociolect that almost becomes a code – a secret language which excludes those not 'in the know'.

---

**ACTIVITY 35**

Suggest how the distinctive slang or jargon associated with the following groups and activities has the effect of excluding those not 'in the know': (1) drugs slang used between dealers and buyers; (2) medical terminology used between doctors as they discuss your condition; (3) computer jargon; and (4) technical terms used by garage mechanics when they explain to you what has gone wrong with your car.

---

# Preparing for the examination

## The examination

The examination for this module of the AQA Specification A lasts $1\frac{1}{2}$ hours. In that time you have to:

- study a selection of short spoken and written extracts

- make connections between and group together some of the texts, as you did in Activity 4

- answer two questions based on these texts, dividing your time equally between them

In your answers you must:

- demonstrate your skills of linguistic analysis

- apply what you have learned about language in this module to the texts on the paper

## Preparing to meet the Assessment Objectives

It is important that your answers meet the relevant Assessment Objectives for this module (see page 1). As you approach the examination, you need to gear your revision of this module to meeting them in full. The table opposite will help you to do this.

| Assessment Objective | This means you need to . . | Revision tip |
|---|---|---|
| 'communicate clearly the knowledge, understanding and insight appropriate to the study of language, using appropriate terminology and accurate and coherent written expression' | . . . write precisely and in some detail about various aspects of the language in the texts, using appropriate linguistic terminology. Write in accurate, clear English, and organise and express your analysis coherently. | Review your personal glossary and the one printed at the end of this book. Make sure you understand and can use the new linguistic terms you have learned. |
| 'know and use key features of frameworks for the systematic study of spoken and written English' | . . . apply a relevant analytical framework to the texts. Be systematic in your approach to the analysis. | Review the different levels of linguistic analysis: discourse structure, form, sentence and grammar, lexis, and sounds and spelling. Revise – and memorise – the stylistics and analysing talk frameworks, and test your analytical skills by applying them to texts you find for yourself. |
| 'understand, discuss and explore concepts and issues relating to language in use' | . . . show how context, audience, purpose and other factors have influenced the way language is used in the texts you analyse. | Revise the relevant parts of this module, and memorise a mental checklist of these factors. |
| 'distinguish, describe and interpret variation in the meanings and forms of spoken and written language according to context' | . . . offer a detailed interpretation of how meanings are conveyed in the texts you analyse. Explain how the contexts of these texts have helped shape their form and meanings. | Review your own analytical exercises and the samples provided in the commentaries. |

## In the exam . . .

### If a question asks you to group texts together

Remember: there is no 'right' combination. The texts chosen could be linked in many ways – but you must justify and explain your suggested groupings by basing your categories on linguistic criteria.

*If a question asks you to analyse individual texts*

Write in precise detail about each one, using appropriate terminology to define precisely how language is used, and explain what factors (audience, context, purpose, etc.) have helped to shape the text.

# Commentaries

## Activity 1

There are many reasons why there is so much variation in English. Historically, English was not a single language but a number of related German dialects brought to this country by invaders from the region of present-day Germany. These ancient differences produced many local variations, and until the twentieth century communities and their dialects remained relatively isolated. Even today, communities may take pride in retaining distinctive voices that express their character and identity. True, the version of English used in the media and taught in schools (Standard English) is often seen as 'correct', but this can be a controversial issue, as we'll discover later.

Speech certainly comes before writing in children's language learning, as it has throughout the history of human society. Spoken language is fundamental to our personal and social lives, yet in our society it seems to be valued less (by our educational and examination systems, for example) than writing. However, although traditional English courses have often been based on the study of literature and the printed word, your English Language course pays at least equal attention to the forms of talk.

The situation described by Ayumi in Query C is one that we all recognise. Each social situation we find ourselves in tends to produce its own distinctive forms of language. So, as we move from one place to another and assume different roles, we adopt the language of the particular social group to which we belong (see the discussion of sociolect on page 42). Nevertheless, as individuals we may still retain our personal linguistic 'fingerprints', so the science fiction scenario suggested in Query D is really not as far-fetched as you might imagine. Although skilled performers like Rory Bremner can produce striking impressions of individuals' voices, the precise combination of tone, pitch, volume and expression that make up an individual's speech can be as distinctive as a fingerprint (see the discussion of idiolect on page 37).

There is no doubt that every language is continually changing – as long as the people and the societies that use it continue to evolve. It is easy to see how developing technologies go on changing language, but this effect is not restricted to vocabulary and grammar. As Kibria indicates, you have only to listen to old BBC news broadcasts or the soundtracks of old films to recognise the changes in spoken English.

Language change does not happen as a result of someone making a decree or passing a law; however, people who have influence, power or authority in society may be more likely to affect the process of language change.

Janet's experience of learning languages is certainly not unusual; most of us find learning a second language far more difficult than acquiring our own mother tongue. This is because we are seldom in the position of infants, totally immersed in the language; neither do we have the same motivation to learn. As children, the need to communicate is vital to our every need. Besides, many British people are deterred from learning a second language by the widespread use of English across the world. It also seems to be true that our receptiveness to new languages and our ability to learn them decline as we grow older.

## Activity 3

Of course, there is no single best way of classifying language in use. In this exercise, you may have decided to categorise according to the purpose or function of language in a given situation (exchanging information, asking questions . . .), the nature of the situation itself (formal or informal, family/school/workplace . . .) or the language medium (phone, Internet . . .). You might also have considered the style of language you would actually use (for example slang, polite, etc.).These are just some of the many valid ways of classifying language.

## Activity 4

The extracts are:

    A: Transcription of a recording made during a lesson.
    B: Transcription of a Tyneside speaker.
    C: The evidence of an eye witness given to the US enquiry into the sinking of the *Titanic* in 1912.
    D: Extract from 'The Passionate Shepherd to his Love' by Christopher Marlowe, late sixteenth century.
    E: Extract from Microsoft Windows 95 installation manual.
    F: Transcript of a radio phone-in programme.
    G: Extract from 'The Jumblies' by Edward Lear, 1871.
    H: Quoted from a speech attributed to John Ball, co-leader of the Peasants' Revolt, 1381.
    I: Quoted from *Sons and Lovers* by D. H. Lawrence, 1913.

How you decided to link pairs of texts will have depended on which aspects you chose to focus on. If you were thinking about the *topic* of the texts, perhaps you linked C with G, because they are both about sinking ships! Alternatively, A and E might be linked as they both involve instruction, and D and H might belong together as persuasive texts – in which case, you were considering *purpose* or *function*. You could just as easily match H with D as belonging to an earlier period in the development of English (using *chronology* as a shared feature), or link A, B and F as examples of *spontaneous* speech, or link B with I as examples of *regional* speech.

Even apparently different texts have things in common: if you paired B and C because both include stories or narratives, or D and G as examples of verse, you were considering the **genre** of the texts. You might even have linked G with A, as they both seem to be aimed at a young audience. Finally, you may have linked texts according to the style of their language, pairing texts like C and D which are written in a rather formal way or noting the technical language in others. This combination of the degree of formality/informality and the kind of vocabulary specific to a particular topic is sometimes referred to as the **register** of a text.

## Activity 8

We have picked out some of the key features of the poem – you may have spotted others. The poem:

- is set out in short lines

- addresses the reader directly, using 'you'

- rhymes

- refers personally to the writer as 'me'

- commands the reader to do something

- has a lot of descriptive language to do with the countryside

- includes the word 'love'

- uses a word that doesn't seem to have the same meaning nowadays (what does it mean to 'prove' pleasures?)

- has a regular rhythm

- uses words in an unusual order ('we will all the pleasures prove', instead of the more usual 'we will prove all the pleasures')

- uses two words ('prove', 'love') that look as if they should rhyme but don't – at least, not nowadays

## Activity 15

This exercise is not as simple as it seems. Some of the texts are dominated by one sentence type – Extracts B and C consist 100% of declaratives and Extract E is made up entirely of imperatives, for example. However, although most of Extract A is giving instructions, it contains some sentences that have a different function ('I'll get you one') and some disguised instructions that start off as declaratives ('what I want you to do please'). A bald series of imperatives (as in Extract E) is seldom used in spoken contexts, as they would sound unduly abrupt and bossy.

## Activity 17

| Key question | Word class investigation |
|---|---|
| Overview | The speech seems designed by John Ball to inspire his listeners to reject the poor conditions under which they are obliged to live and to revolt against the wealthy. |
| How much of the text conveys facts and how much conveys opinions? Is the language emotional or detached? | As a persuasive speech, it has few facts and bases its appeal on emotions and opinions. The adjective 'unjust' describes the actions of the rich and powerful. Ball describes the poor (his audience) as having good hearts and compares them to good husbands (meaning 'farmers') in contrast to the evil weeds that represent the 'naughty men', the great (as in powerful) lords of the realm. However, it is the nouns that most clearly convey the speaker's opinions and emotions. The terms 'bondage', 'servitude' and 'oppression' are all used to describe the peasants' condition and belong to the same semantic field. Just as good and evil are contrasted, so are these terms contrasted with the liberty Ball wishes to claim, and the weeds contrasted with the corn. As this speech is very much about feelings and ideas, many of the nouns are abstract – but by using the concrete nouns 'weeds', 'corn' and 'yoke', Ball makes his meanings clear and forces his listeners to imagine themselves as farm animals weighed down by a tremendous burden. |
| Does the text seem personal or impersonal? | The speaker uses the first person plural 'we' and 'our' to unite himself with his listeners, and introduces himself with 'I' to use his personal authority in his appeal. Finally, by using the second person forms 'you' and 'ye' he addresses his audience directly. |
| Is it formal/neutral/ informal? Is it simple or sophisticated? Does it include words that belong to a particular subject or theme, or that are specialist, technical, literary or old-fashioned? | Although personal in tone, the speech seems quite formal with verbs such as 'exhort', 'bethink' and 'counsel' belonging to a rather literary register. The concrete nouns – 'yoke', 'ground', 'weeds', 'corn' – are drawn from an agricultural register very familiar to the peasant audience. Of course, we recognise in the text features that alert us to its age – there are nouns and adjectives whose meanings seem to have changed ('naughty', 'husband', 'common'), other words which are unfamiliar today ('bethink', 'questmongers'), different |

| Are there any non-standard or regional expressions? | pronoun forms ('ye'), and verbs behaving differently ('riddeth' and 'tilleth'). |
| Is language being used in its literal sense – or does it use similes and/or metaphors and other figurative expressions? | Figurative language is used to convey abstract ideas using concrete images. As well as comparing the bondage of his listeners to a yoke, Ball compares the peasants' rebellion to the actions of a good husband (farmer), who in overthrowing the rich and powerful is doing no more than getting rid of a few weeds for the good of the corn (that is, the prosperity of the whole country). |

## Activity 22

| *Starts with a broad overview of the context of the ad – all points to be related to this.* | This advert attempts to persuade its target audience, young music fans living an active social lifestyle, to buy the CDfender, a device to protect CDs from damage. It seems to speak directly to readers, using a number of witty plays on words and references to popular groups and TV programmes to amuse the readers and invite them to identify with the situation described in the ad. |
| *First detailed points at Level 1 – discourse structure* | It uses a problem–solution structure typical of many adverts. First, the image and the first part of the text present the problem (messed-up CDs), which it hopes readers will recognise; then, it offers the 'solution' in the shape of the CDfender product. |
| *Now at Level 2 – form. Do you agree? Or is there another suggestion about the typeface used?* | The impact of the ad is largely visual, with the text reinforcing a large image of the leaky curry carton on the original ad. The paragraphing of the text (in two columns) is irregular, but most 'paragraphs' are, in fact, only single sentences, making for easily digestible reading. The typeface of the eye-catching slogan 'Curry on the House' may suggest a poster for a dance music gig. |
| *Moving to Level 3 – sentences* *questions used persuasively rather than requiring an actual answer.* | The ad is composed mainly of declarative sentences that describe either (a) the causes of the problem or (b) the qualities of the solution. However, it includes two rhetorical questions* – 'So how do you stop your |

*Note how the evidence is quoted using dashes and brackets.*

favourite hip hop hopping all over the place? Or your Garbage sounding rubbish?' – to which the only answer is going to be – by buying this product! It also includes an imperative, which forces the reader to imagine having bought the product and emphasises how easy it is to use – 'Just peel off the backing and press CDefender on the disc'. Many of the sentences do not look like conventional 'written sentences' – beginning with 'Or', 'And' and just consisting in one case of a phrase ('With CDfender').This makes the text feel more like speech than writing – as if the advertiser is talking to us directly.

*Level 4 – lexis*
*Each point needs illustrating – but single words or very short phrases are all that you need to quote here.*
*\*pun – a deliberate play on two or more possible meanings of a word or phrase.*

The advert uses some nouns that reinforces the idea of 'mess' (fag ash, beer, sticky ends). These, and the references throughout to groups and types of music ('House or garage, jungle or country') imply a certain kind of lifestyle which helps identify the likely audience/market for the product, but they also help create an informal register ('fag') and humour by playing on words ('sticky ends'). The proper nouns referring to groups ('Cardigans', 'Ash', 'Garbage' etc.) and the music types ('House or garage, jungle or country') continue the puns* that constantly play on two possible meanings of a word/phrase. The 'in' reference to Kenny, without directly referring to the programme 'South Park', confirms the target audience for the product. The ad makes humorous comparisons: (1) 'as squeaky clean as The Corrs', and (2) 'It can stay put longer than a crusty's socks'. These (1) keep the musical theme and (2) draw on a slightly vulgar youthful register.

By contrast, the ad also contains some technical language ('It's an optical quality polycarbonate film') to convince us of the technological nature of the product.

*Level 5 – phonology and orthography*

The ad includes some interesting use of non-standard spellings. The product name itself – 'CDfender' – is a neat amalgam of CD and defender, exploiting the sound of the letter 'd'. Then it imitates the actual sticking and jumping of a damaged CD in the way the words 'sticks' and 'jumps' are presented.

Overall, the ad uses a variety of linguistic devices to attract the attention of its target audience and promote the product effectively.

## Activity 23

- Some features missing from the transcript are: (1) the speaker's facial expressions, hand gestures and body language (these physical aspects, which contribute to the meanings of speech, are called **paralinguistic features**); (2) the actual sound and tone of her voice (this includes the way her voice moves up and down as she speaks – the **intonation** – the stress placed on particular words and the tempo of the speech. These aspects of the way our voices and manner of speaking add to our meanings are referred to as **prosodic features**. Their absence makes it difficult to judge the speaker's mood, attitude and feelings about the events she describes.

- The elements of the spoken account most obviously missing from the written statement are the hesitations and **fillers** that occur in spontaneous speech. These may be verbal ('you know', 'like') or non-verbal ('er', 'um'). The written statement also avoids the digressions (the witness's dog-walking) that appear in the spoken version.

- The spoken version seems to consist of long continuous sentences that include breath pauses and the conjunctions 'and', 'but' and 'so'. These are called compound sentences. Sentence boundaries are generally less clear in speech – it is not always easy to say when one sentence stops and the next starts – so it is usual to indicate pauses in transcriptions using (.) or (–) instead of conventional punctuation.

- The inexplicit references work in speech because both the speaker and the listener are physically near the places referred to. This is a significant aspect of speech – that many of its meanings are context-related. In writing we cannot expect our readers to share the same context, so our meanings need to be explicit and context-free.

- In her spoken account, the speaker uses verbs to sensationalise events, describing the car as 'racing' and the smoke as 'pouring'. At some points, the speaker uses verbs in the present tense – 'this car comes racing down', 'so as I turned round, there's black smoke pouring out' – even though the events are in the past. This is a common feature of spoken narratives – it is as if the speaker is bringing events alive by re-enacting them in the present.

- The spoken version contains an example of regional, non-standard grammar ('I were') and several colloquial expressions like 'bloody great crash' and 'some poor bugger', which have been replaced in the written version, making it generally more formal and precise.

## Activity 25

Examples you may have suggested include *ea* as in 'eat', 'feat' and 'beat'; *ie* as in 'siege'; *ei* as in 'receive'; *e* with final 'e' as in 'Pete'; *ae* as in 'encyclopaedia'; and *e* as in 'Peking'.

## Activity 26

Some places certainly seem to limit the range of roles you can take and the things you can say. You may have discussed the differences between the way you act in your own home and when visiting someone else's. As a 'host' you may assume more of a leader's role with a group of friends; in church you are unlikely to feel it appropriate to tell a joke to the person next to you; at work, especially if you are involved with the public, you are likely to behave with more respect towards complete strangers than you would in other situations.

However, when the question of where you are is combined with who you are with, the limitations become even clearer. You may have thought about gender – how an all male, all female, or mixed company influences the way you talk. Equally interesting is the question of relative status – whether, in any particular situation, you seem to enjoy a dominant role (with younger brothers and sisters, or with friends, perhaps), you are more or less equal to your conversational partner, or the situation places you in a subordinate role (say, in the classroom, with parents or at work). In each case, the different role you play determines whether you ask questions, crack jokes, use formal or colloquial language, or make an effort to soften your natural regional accent in the interests of formality.

Where the purpose of talk is very clearly defined – for example, a customer buying a CD from a music shop – the exchange becomes very predictable. Interviewers ask questions to find the best person for the job, stand-up comedians tell jokes to make us laugh, and doctors ask us questions to diagnose an illness. We would be surprised if any of these people digressed from the style of language that their situation requires.

## Activity 27

### Student's notes

The talk begins with the DJ cueing in the caller. This places him 'in charge' of the interview. He also uses her first name, assuming some familiarity and informality, and an informal greeting. Tanya replies, using the same informal greeting, but allows the DJ to continue to take the lead with what sounds like a catch-phrase but is also her next cue. Tanya replies, echoing the DJ's words, coming straight to the point but with some hesitation – perhaps as a result of nervousness?

The DJ attempts to interrupt – a bit rude? Broadcasters often try to do this. But Tanya carries on. When she has finished, the DJ now succeeds in getting in his question. Humorous, informal use of 'lump'. Repeats 'Canada'.

Again, some hesitation from Tanya, before a straight reply. The 'lead' in the talk is the DJ. The DJ offers a comment on Tanya's answer – makes her feel good? Like a teacher? False start – personal comment to suggest has shared interest. Phrases next question.

Tanya offers agreement – supportive – but slightly overlaps, forcing the DJ to repeat part of question.

## Activity 28

Your parents – or anyone else closely involved in your upbringing – were your earliest and, for much of your pre-school life, your main influences. They provided you with much of the 'data' on which you based your earliest guesses at how English works. You probably imitated not just the words and phrases you heard them use, but also their intonation patterns and accents. At an early stage, you may also have learned notions of what was acceptable or unacceptable usage in terms of 'good' or 'bad' English, or swear-words considered taboo.

However, once you started going to school, the linguistic influence of your parents probably diminished steadily as they competed with many other and increasingly powerful factors in your life. In your A2 course, you will go on to study in some detail the processes of early language acquisition and the role that parents have in this.

The places where you lived may have influenced you in ways that you were entirely unaware of at the time. The most obvious aspect of your speech, one that may reveal your geographical origins, is your accent; this term is used to describe the way you pronounce the phonemes of English, and the distinctive intonation patterns that accompany your speech. You may also use words, phrases and unusual grammatical constructions characteristic of a region, collectively known as dialect (see page 38).

If you have moved from one place to another you may have adjusted your speech, consciously or unconsciously, to fit in with your new surroundings and, as a result, significantly changed your accent/dialect.

Teachers will certainly have had some influence – introducing many new words and encouraging you to develop your language skills throughout your educational career. They may also have been strong influences in developing your sense of what is 'correct' or 'acceptable' English – though despite years of such influence, outside the classroom you probably still use language in ways they may well disapprove of! In school, the linguistic influence of groups of friends is soon likely to outstrip that of either parents or teachers. Your need to be accepted by your peers is likely to have led you to use similar speech to the friends you most wish to be like – so your accent may have become more like your friends' than your parents' and your speech may have begun to include the playground slang or swear-words that parents and teachers tried in vain to discourage. Some groups may develop slang words unique to them, or share particular catch-phrases which become 'in words'.

TV, music and other media no doubt became an increasing influence as you got older. Phrases adopted from the Australian English of *Neighbours*, or the street slang of Gangsta Rap, may have started to feature in the vocabulary of you and your friends. This is likely to affect accent and grammar, too; phrases borrowed from such sources may include non-standard constructions, and some definitely non-RP pronunciations.

As you grow older, you encounter a new set of linguistic influences when you enter the world of work. The way you are obliged to use language when serving burgers, selling shoes or talking with fellow workers on a building site may involve you with a kind of jargon, a different kind of slang, or speaking in an accent slightly different from your usual one. To start with, this influence may not extend far beyond your workplace, but as adult life progresses it is likely to have an increasingly strong effect on your individual language use.

## Activity 30

*Pronunciation.* It is difficult to tell from a transcript exactly how a speaker sounds. On the basis of the imperfect information presented here, you would probably note the shortened *mi* for 'my' and some extended vowel sounds (*waar* for 'war' and *weel* for 'well'). He also pronounces 'no' more like the Scottish 'nae'.

*Vocabulary.* The speaker's vocabulary includes a number of words we do not recognise as Standard English. Amongst these, 'bairn' is commonly used in the north of England and in Scotland for child; 'clarts' to mean mud is rather less common, and is restricted mainly to the north-east of England. 'Bourn' and 'beck' are two alternatives for small streams, while 'ket' in the north and east can refer to snacks or sweets. Oddly, the same word can also mean rubbish in parts of Cumbria and Yorkshire! 'Gan' for go is common throughout the north-east, whereas 'hoy' is rather more limited to the Tyne and Wear region. (*Source*: Upton, Sanderson and Widdowson, *Word Maps: A Dialect Atlas of England*, Croom Helm, 1987.)

*Grammar.* As far as grammar is concerned, you may have been surprised to find that the speaker generally uses Standard English constructions. The exceptions mainly concern the verb 'do' and its use in the formation of the question 'does tha want to know' (Standard English 'do you want to know') and the negative statement 'tha disn'y know'. There is also an example of what linguists call a **double negative** construction in the phrase 'we never had nowt' (Standard English 'we didn't have/never had anything') – a feature of many regional dialects – and a non-standard prepositional phrase in 'on a night' (Standard English 'at night').

## Activity 33

It would not be surprising if you decided that none of these expressions was 'good' grammar; by definition, none of them belongs to the grammatical structures of Standard English and therefore, in many people's eyes, they are not correct or proper English. Whereas people seem happy to accept that dialects preserve an interesting lexical diversity, the view has taken root that dialect grammar is a corruption of 'proper' English grammar, and that thousands of people in a particular region must somehow be making grammatical 'mistakes' whenever they speak.

However, this is a misguided view. No less than its lexis, a dialect's grammatical system is rooted in that dialect's history – and far from being incorrect or corrupt versions of what we now know as Standard English, dialects have enjoyed a parallel development to the prestige variety of the language. As you will learn in your A2 course, the notion of Standard English that emerged gradually from the fifteenth to the eighteenth centuries was based largely on the speech of those who happened to enjoy some education, influence and power in the south-east of England. By the eighteenth century a clear notion of 'correctness' established itself, with the effect that other dialects were increasingly castigated as inferior or uneducated.

## Activity 34

Your family may well have some words which are used in ways that outsiders might not recognise, perhaps because they arose from incidents in the past or other aspects of family life. Many families have rituals that involve certain phrases being said at certain times (such as birthdays and Christmas). Everyone's examples will be different.

Your immediate group of friends may have certain favourite 'buzzwords' or slang, or use swear-words in particular ways. You may be influenced by catch-phrases from favourite films, TV programmes or music, which you subsequently introduce into your conversation. There may even be a favoured accent – and newcomers to the group may end up altering their speech in this direction in order to fit in.

People who live in your town or region will share some aspects of accent and pronunciation, as well as some dialect vocabulary and non-standard English grammatical constructions. People who share a particular interest and people who do the same job are most likely to share a specialist vocabulary or jargon that is specific to the interest or job. People from the same social background may also share some linguistic features. The relationship between the social class we belong to and the accent, dialect and style of our speech is a complex and often controversial one which is covered in more detail in Module 2, Language and Social Contexts. In general, people from working class backgrounds do tend to use a higher proportion of regional accent/dialect features than those from professional or middle class backgrounds.

People who like the same kind of music may also share a common language, based not only on references to the bands and music itself but because different styles of music (dance, metal, indie, etc.) are part of a wider subculture characterised by distinctive uses of language. Even people who support the same team often form close-knit groups; the language they use, such as the banter and chanting of a football crowd or the written language of fanzines, helps to cement this tribal solidarity.

# MODULE (2) Language and Social Contexts

This module counts for 35% of the AS qualification, or $17\frac{1}{2}$% of the total A Level marks.

---

## ASSESSMENT OBJECTIVES

The skills and knowledge that you develop in this module, and that will be tested in the examination you take at the end of it, are defined by the examination board's Assessment Objectives. These require that you:

- communicate clearly the knowledge, understanding and insight appropriate to the study of language, using appropriate terminology and accurate and coherent written expression
  (5% of the final AS mark; $2\frac{1}{2}$% of the final A Level mark)

- know and use key features of frameworks for the systematic study of spoken and written English
  (10% of the final AS mark; 5% of the final A Level mark)

- understand, discuss and explore concepts and issues relating to language in use
  (10% of the final AS mark; 5% of the final A Level mark)

- distinguish, describe and interpret variation in the meanings and forms of spoken and written language according to context
  (10% of the final AS mark; 5% of the final A Level mark)

---

## Introduction

In the previous module, you started to understand the variations in the ways that English is used all around us. You also learned that there are different ways of describing and analysing language use, and began to apply a number of analytical frameworks to this task. In this module, you will continue this approach as you meet a number of spoken and written texts, but here the focus is on how our language is shaped by social factors.

It is hard to overstate the importance of language in allowing us to develop as social beings. Some evolutionary biologists have suggested that a uniquely human capacity for language developed alongside the ability to organise ourselves into increasingly sophisticated social groupings and to collaborate in the evolutionary struggle for survival and development. Indeed, it is virtually impossible to consider the meanings of a spoken or written text without fully considering the social contexts in which it is produced.

This means thinking about:

- who produces it

- why it has been produced

- the relationship between the author/producer and the receiver/audience

- the place and time in which it was produced

In this area of language studies we try to answer a very basic but far-reaching question: how does our use of language reflect the way our society is organised?

In particular, we will use the following key concepts and frameworks to explore how social context affects language use:

*lexis*: the range of vocabulary available to speakers of a language

*grammar*: all aspects of the structures and functions of a language

*phonology/phonetics*: the vocal aspects of language, such as intonation, rhythm, pace, volume and stress in spoken English

*semantics*: the ways in which meanings are communicated in language

*pragmatics*: the ways in which social messages/relations and implied meanings are conveyed in language

 It may be useful to review some of the relevant aspects of language use we touched on in Module 1. These include:

'A question of language', query A, page 3; 'Accents and dialects', pages 38–41: variations in English accents and dialects, and the ways in which these different forms are often regarded as unequal in value and status.

'A question of language', query C, page 3: the variations in our own use of language according to the social contexts we are in, and especially the particular language styles demanded by different kinds of occupational situation.

'Using the stylistics framework', pages 13–30: a systematic approach to describing and analysing language styles in different contexts.

'A framework for analysing talk', pages 34–5: ways of examining examples of conversation in transcription, and asking key questions about the way we behave in different conversational contexts.

'Fitting in: language as a membership card', page 42: the ways in which distinctive uses of language (sociolects) can indicate that we belong to (or are excluded from) certain social groups.

# Starting to explore

In this module, we build on many of these ideas and also introduce some new ones. The next few activities help you begin to ask the kinds of question you will be investigating later in the module.

Let's start by considering how we all vary our language according to the social context we are in at any one time. We can call this variation in an individual's use of language their language repertoire.

Read the following brief pen portrait of Charlotte Johnson, aged 34:

Charlotte was brought up on the outskirts of Manchester and attended her local comprehensive school before studying Business at Birmingham University. Her parents are both white and have lived their lives in the north of England; her father was a factory worker, her mother a shop assistant. Eight years ago Charlotte married Ray, an accountant from Essex whom she met at University, and they now live in London with their twins Emma and Jack, aged 7. She is the Personnel Manager at a local retail store, which involves being part of the store management team and dealing with staff recruitment, training and appraisal. In her spare time she enjoys playing squash, and occasionally she manages to meet up with a couple of her old school friends who also live and work in London.

## ACTIVITY 1      C3.1A/B

Now discuss your responses to the following questions, using the table to record your speculations:

- How might the style of language Charlotte uses vary in the course of a typical week?

- What factors might influence these variations?

| Context | Language style | Influences |
|---|---|---|
| At work | | |
| With her friends | | |
| With her parents | | |
| At home | | |

Compare your responses with the commentary on page 95.

## ACTIVITY 2

C3.1A

First remind yourself of the questions we used in Module 1 (pages 34–5) for analysing talk.

Examine the following transcript of a telephone conversation. Deduce from it anything you can about the participants, their relationship, and the purpose of the call. In particular, try to define the role that each speaker is playing, and their relative importance or status. Record your discussion in note form.

(The symbol // marks a point when two speakers talk at the same time; (.) marks a short breath pause; and (4) marks a longer pause of approximately 4 seconds' duration.)

A: [Scots accent] Good morning (.) you're through to XX Customer Service and my name's Adam (.) How may I help you

C: [RP accent] Ah, hello (.) it's about a redirection request that seems to be causing a few problems

A: I see sir (.) could I take your customer reference number please

C: Yeah (3.) it's 543 (.) 986 (.) 674 (.) PY

A: (4) That's (.) Mr Brown

C: That's correct

A: Of 57 Jackson Avenue

C: That's it

A: And what seems to be the problem sir

C: Well to be honest I'm getting a bit fed up having to explain the same thing over and over again (.) I've tried three times now to get this sorted out but // it seems to be impossible to

A: // Oh

C: arrange a simple redirection without (.) well (.)

A: // mm

C: // spending hours and hours trying to get through

A: I'm very sorry to hear that sir (.) can I just confirm a few details and I'm sure I'll be able to sort // things out for you

C: // I've already given my name, number and shoe size to the last person I spoke to before getting cut off

Compare your analysis with the commentary on page 95.

What emerges from these preliminary discussions is that there are many questions we need to ask about how our use of language is related to social factors. We can sum these up under three headings:

**How does language in use reflect the different status and position of individuals and groups in society?** We consider this question under the heading 'Language and power' (page 61).

How might any differences between men's and women's roles in society, and our attitudes towards them, be reflected in language use? We consider this question under the heading 'Language and gender' (page 84).

How does the language used by people in particular occupations identify them and reflect their professional context, values and attitudes? We consider this question under the heading 'Language and occupational groups' (page 90).

## Language and power

Whenever groups of people gather together, create organisations or interact, we quickly become aware that some people are able to exercise more influence and authority than others. In situations or organisations where we are aware of differences in status, such as in the family or at work, we may take for granted these inequalities in influence and authority. However, even among groups of apparently 'equal' friends or workmates, some individuals may seem to have more clout or influence than others, and this may be reflected in how language is used within the group.

### ACTIVITY 3

Let's consider how far this is true for some of the groups you belong to. For each of the groups listed below – or any others you belong to – order the members of the group in terms of their status or influence within it:

- your family
- the group of friends you socialise with most
- the people at your place of work

In our society, power and influence may be enjoyed by certain individuals (the Prime Minister, your mother or father, the head teacher, Rupert Murdoch), by groups of people (a trade union, a pressure group, the police), or even by entire nations (the United States, Russia).

### ACTIVITY 4                                                                C3.1A

In a group, try to agree on a list of the five most powerful individuals and groups of people in Britain. Then try to agree which of the following enjoy more power and influence in our society in general terms:

- white people, or people belonging to other ethnic groups
- men, or women
- business managers, or those working for them
- people who help run the media (TV and newspapers), or people who buy or subscribe to media products or programmes
- people in the north of Britain, or people in the south

Explain your choices before comparing the outcomes of your discussion with the commentary on page 96.

Whatever conclusions you reached in Activity 4, you may have started to ask where power comes from. You may have considered the relative importance of:

- individual strength of personality: like that possessed by the extrovert 'leader' of a group of friends

- profession or occupation: a police officer has power because of the uniform, not because of who she or he is

- social class or background: someone from a well-off family or with a good education may have some advantages

- gender: men still have more influence than women in many areas

- ethnic origins: white British people may still enjoy more power than people from Asian, Caribbean and other non-white backgrounds

- wealth and economic power: rich people exert their power in all sorts of ways

- political power: politicians clearly enjoy the power to shape policies and pass laws

With all this in mind, we must now return to the raw material of our study – language – and begin to explore the ways in which these inequalities of power and influence are reflected in the variety of English in use and our attitudes towards it.

## The accents and dialects of English

In Module 1 we briefly considered the variety of accents and dialects to be found in Britain, and the attitudes commonly held towards some of these. In particular, we saw how the dialect we call Standard English has come to be regarded as the model of 'correct' English, and that the non-regional accent known as Received Pronunciation (RP) enjoys similar prestige as the 'proper' way to talk.

Read the following article, 'Putting the accent on a North Mouth Divide'. It originally appeared in the early 1990s in the *Northern Echo*, a regional newspaper published in the north-east of England:

## PUTTING THE ACCENT ON A NORTH MOUTH DIVIDE

THE VOICE on the television advert persuading you to buy bread, beer or crisps probably sounds familiar.

For market researchers associate these products with the North-East accent and qualities of being friendly, down-to-earth – and undynamic.

But the man selling flash cars, holidays or pension schemes is likely to have a southern accent because advert makers say it denotes ambition, authority and intelligence.

Now speech coaches say many Northern businessmen are trying to change the way they speak because they feel they are not taken seriously enough.

As one (southern-based) national newspaper summed it up: 'Northerners are rushing to prove they are not as thick as the accent that marks them out.'

It is just the latest example of an increasing North Mouth Divide which is threatening to stifle strong regional accents.

And language experts argued that the trend should be strongly resisted.

York University lecturer Dr John Local said: 'The media use accents all the time in subtle ways. But it is hard to say with this kind of thing whether the media lead or follow.'

---

### ACTIVITY 5                                                                     C3.1A/B

Carry out your own survey of accents in TV advertisements during an evening's viewing, and present your findings to the class. Your survey should ask: (1) What kinds of products are advertised by using different regional accents? (2) What kinds of products are advertised using mainly RP accents? Is it true that these tend to be 'high prestige' products? (3) How do some adverts use both regional and RP speech? Consider, for example, how often RP voices provide the voice over or the last word in an advert that also uses regional speakers on-screen.

The article's closing sentence raises the question of how far the media are to blame for the perpetuation of these stereotypes. In the light of your findings, try to agree which of the following statements most accurately describes the role of the media in their use of regional accents:

- the media simply reflect stereotypes that already exist in society

- the media help reinforce and strengthen social stereotypes

- the media create and spread stereotypes

In considering these issues, you may like refer to the following review of a book by Dr J. Honey, *Does Accent Matter?* In this extract, reviewer D. J. Enright summarises some of the research findings reported in Honey's book:

Experimental research shows that RP heads the prestige league (its speakers are even reckoned to be handsomer, taller, cleaner), followed by Scottish (Edinburgh), Welsh and Irish (kept within bounds), while Cockney, Scouse, Glaswegian, West Midlands and Belfast come bottom.

Yorkshire is relatively well thought of, as the language of farmers and cricketers, and so are rustic accents, a fact ascribed here to the nineteenth-century worship of the countryside. Unattributed theories put *Scouse* down to the prevalence of adenoids and Glaswegian to ill-fitting false teeth.

We can extend our study of accents in the media to include news broadcasts, so often cited as an example of 'proper English'. National newsreaders almost invariably speak using an RP accent, and even readers of the local news tend to have only the gentlest hint of a regional accent in their speech. Why is this?

The following may help you answer this question. It is an account of a much-quoted experiment carried out in the 1970s by the researcher Howard Giles:

## THE WORK OF HOWARD GILES

In the 1970s a team of researchers led by Howard Giles carried out a number of research experiments called matched guise experiments, designed to test people's responses to different accents. In one of these, Giles delivered two identical presentations on a controversial topic to different groups of Midlands sixth-form students using RP with one group and the local regional accent with the other. Afterwards, he surveyed his audiences for their opinions of his intelligence and knowledge. The students who had heard the presentation in RP rated his intelligence and authoritativeness considerably higher than those he had addressed in the regional accent.

## ACTIVITY 6

Bear in mind the results of Giles's experiment as you consider which of the following statements offers the most likely explanation for the universal use of RP among newsreaders. Place them in your rank order of importance, then compare your findings with the commentary on page 96.

**RP and the news**

| Explanation | Rank order |
| --- | --- |
| All newsreaders went to similar kinds of schools and had a similar education, so they all have a similar accent | |
| Not everyone would be able to understand the broadcasts if they used regional accents | |
| People would find the news less believable and take it less seriously if it was spoken in a regional accent | |

## Accent and social class

The accent of English we seem to respect the most happens to be the one that is used principally by middle class, university educated people working in professional occupations. In other words, RP's unique status is largely due to its being the accent of the powerful. RP has what linguists sometimes describe as **overt prestige** – an 'official' status that most speakers seem to be consciously aware of.

In fact, the relationship between our accent and our social background is complex. Researchers have carried out surveys to explore this relationship; one frequently quoted study was reported by Peter Trudgill in his book *Sociolinguistics: An Introduction to Language and Society*. Here is a summary of the findings of an investigation he carried out into the regional accent in Norwich:

Trudgill decided to concentrate on three distinct phonetic features of the Norwich accent: the tendency to say *n* rather than *ng* in words like 'running', use of the glottal stop (a distinctive pronunciation of the *t* sound in the middle of words like 'bottle'), and the absence of an *h* sound at the beginning of words like 'hairy'. He found that the percentage of people using these features in their speech varied with their different social backgrounds (defined in terms of occupation):

|  | % use | | |
|---|---|---|---|
|  | n | t (glottal stop) | h |
| Middle classes (professional occupations) | 31 | 41 | 6 |
| Lower middle classes (clerical and white collar work) | 42 | 62 | 14 |
| Upper working classes (skilled manual work/crafts) | 87 | 89 | 10 |
| Middle working classes (semi-skilled workers) | 95 | 92 | 59 |
| Lower working classes (unskilled labour) | 100 | 94 | 61 |

## ACTIVITY 7

What conclusions can you reasonably draw from Trudgill's data? Write some statements in which you describe the relationships between social class and the use of regional accent in Norwich.

Always be cautious when suggesting such conclusions; remember, this is only one set of data based on a limited sample of speakers. When formulating your conclusions, use expressions like 'tend to', 'appear to', 'seem to', 'are likely to' and 'may' to express an element of tentativeness and uncertainty.

Compare your findings with the commentary on page 97.

Some recent research suggests that the association of RP speech with education, authority and power may be slipping. Other accents may be gaining ground, as reported in this article from *The Times* of 10 September 1998:

# WHY PROPER ENGLISH IS NO LONGER A SHORE THING

Shifts in pronunciations mean that hardly anybody is left who speaks 'proper' English and people such as Tony Blair adjust their accent to suit their audience, a specialist in phonetics and linguistics told a meeting yesterday.

Professor John Wells of University College, London noted that 'Tuesday' has become 'chooseday', 'sure' now sounds identical to 'shore' and it is no longer true that all educated people speak with Received Pronunciation, the traditional tones of the elite.

Estuary English, the speech of London and the South East, is gradually influencing RP, he said. Mr Blair 'demonstrated that he could move downmarket' when he used Estuary tones in an interview with Des O'Connor on television. This was an example of trying to fit in with people by adopting their accents.

This reported increase in the status of non-RP accents compares interestingly with a well-known study carried out by the American researcher William Labov into developments in the local accent on Martha's Vineyard, a resort island off the eastern coast of the United States. During the 1960s and 1970s, the island had become increasingly popular as a resort among relatively affluent middle class New Yorkers. Labov was interested in tracing the impact of these incomers, who generally spoke with an accent close to the US equivalent of the educated prestige RP accent.

## ACTIVITY 8                                                                C3.1A/B

In groups, suggest which of the following developments in Martha's Vineyard would be most likely, and give your reasons:

- Over time, more of the younger people on the island would start to soften their distinctive Martha's Vineyard accent and begin to speak more like the visitors.

- There would probably be very little change.

- The younger people on the island would start to strengthen their regional accent.

Present and justify your suggestions to the class, then turn to the commentary on page 97 to find out what Labov actually discovered.

## Dialects, Standard English, correctness and class

So far, we have considered variations in English accents. When we widen the enquiry to look at dialectal variation too (that is, different vocabulary and grammatical constructions used in regional speech), the issues become even more controversial, especially when they centre on the importance of Standard English and the notion of correctness.

### ACTIVITY 9

Why is it necessary for us to have a standard vocabulary and grammar of English for all speakers? In groups, discuss your responses to this question; try to suggest at least five social factors. List your responses and present them to the class, then compare your list with the commentary on page 98.

For most of us, Standard English means the vocabulary laid down in good dictionaries, and the grammar of 'correct' English as taught in schools, used in books and broadcast by news media.

However, only a relatively small number of us actually use exclusively Standard English; many of us also include in our speech words, expressions and constructions that are part of our regional dialects, as the following *Guardian* article from April 1998 makes clear:

## CHILDREN USING GEATT WORDS INSTEAD OF STANDARD ENGLISH 'IS DEAD WRONG'

Children may choose not to speak properly even when they have a clear knowledge of standard English, a report for the Government's main curriculum quango said yesterday.

Tape recordings made of 11 and 15-year-olds in four regions of England revealed that many speakers used phrases such as 'They have fell out of the picture' or 'It could have came in the window' at the same time as standard English.

The most common wrong usage was of 'there is' followed by a plural. In the south-west, children used 'them books' or 'they books', when they meant 'those books'.

On Merseyside, 'dead' meant 'very' as in 'dead good', on Tyneside 'geatt' was a versatile alternative to 'really', as in 'do it up geatt tight' or 'it's a geatt 20 miles'.

Richard Hudson, of University College, London, who analysed the speech of more than 350 children taped in class eight years ago, found that a third used no non-standard English at all, and that girls used fewer non-standard forms.

'Our evidence may indicate that mere exposure is not sufficient, and that some kind of direct teaching or encouragement is needed', Professor Hudson said.

## ACTIVITY 10

Discuss and consider the following issues raised by this article, writing down your findings before comparing your ideas with the commentary on page 98:

- What reasons might children have for deliberately avoiding Standard English forms?

- What reasons are there to be either concerned or unconcerned that children are not using Standard English?

As with variations in accents, people have often suggested that there is a relationship between the social background of speakers and the non-standard features they use in their speech. Here, then, is another set of findings from Peter Trudgill, who in this study considered one notable aspect of the Norwich dialect: the preference of some speakers for forms such as 'she drive too fast' rather than the Standard English 'she drives too fast'.

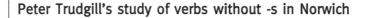

### Peter Trudgill's study of verbs without -s in Norwich

The diagram shows the percentage of speakers in each social class who use this form in their speech:

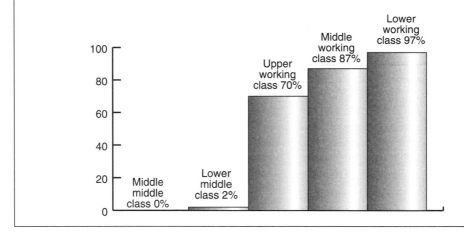

## ACTIVITY 11

Discusss and write down any conclusions which you think you can reasonably draw from Trudgill's data, remembering to be cautious and tentative as you were in Activity 7. Then compare this study with Trudgill's earlier one on accent (page 65). Is the non-standard dialectal speech more distinctive or less distinctive of social class than the accent features?

Compare your responses with the commentary on page 98.

To sum up: the dialect we call Standard English is a necessary common language with overt prestige, whereas non-standard varieties of English are associated with geographical regions and working class speech. In other words, Standard English is the dialect of power.

## Language and ethnic identity

So far, the non-standard dialects we have considered have been associated with different regions. However, there are other varieties of English that are more associated with particular ethnic groups. One example of this is the variety derived from the language of the Caribbean – sometimes referred to as Patois, Creole or Black (British) English.

The poem reprinted below, 'Listen Mr Oxford don' by John Agard, illustrates some of the features of these varieties, and also raises some challenging issues in the area of language and power:

Me not no Oxford don
me a simple immigrant
from Clapham Common
I didn't graduate
I immigrate

But listen Mr Oxford don
I'm a man on de run
and a man on de run
is a dangerous one

I ent have no gun
I ent have no knife
But mugging de Queen's English
is the story of my life

I don/ t need no axe
To split/ up yu syntax
I don/ t need no hammer
To mash/ up yu grammar

I warning you Mr Oxford don
I'm a wanted man
and a wanted man
is a dangerous one

Dem accuse me of assault
on de Oxford dictionary/
imagine a concise peaceful man like me/
dem want me serve time
for inciting rhyme to riot
but I tekking it quiet
down here in Clapham Common

I'm not a violent man Mr Oxford don
I only armed wit mih human breath
but human breath
is a dangerous weapon

So mek dem send one big word after me
I ent serving no jail sentence
I slashing suffix in self-defence
I bashing future wit present tense
and if necessary

I making de Queen's English accessory/
to my offence

## ACTIVITY 12

List some examples of the distinctive features of this variety of English. Then
suggest a Standard English equivalent and try to describe the feature(s)
linguistically. Use the table as a guide, adding further examples to the one
already given:

| Example | Standard English equivalent | Linguistic description |
| --- | --- | --- |
| Me not no Oxford don | I am not an Oxford don (lecturer) | (1) Different first person pronoun; (2) absent verb 'be' (= 'am') form; (3) double negative |

Suggest and note down what you think this poem is saying about the
status/power of Standard English (or RP). Then compare your responses with the
commentary on page 99.

Varieties of English such as Agard's and our many regional dialects are often
dismissed as 'poor English', 'lazy English' or just plain 'ungrammatical'. It is all
too easy to see forms of Caribbean-derived English and regional dialects as a
simplified or corrupted form of the language. This way of looking at non-
standard varieties of the language is sometimes called a **Deficit Model**. On the
face of it, some of the most notable features of Creole seem to add up to a
simplification of English grammar, especially in the endings we often find on
words to indicate tense ('walk', 'walked') and person ('I walk', 'he walks'). Many
of these grammatical endings – or **inflections** as they are called – are not
present in Creole speech.

It is also true that Creole forms started out in life as simple languages with very
basic grammars designed to enable speakers of different languages to
communicate. Such forms are referred to as pidgins. However, when a pidgin
becomes the adopted mother tongue of a community, as happened with
Caribbean pidgins during the slave era, it invariably develops in complexity as a
language in its own right. So, a closer inspection of Creole grammar may lead us
to a conclusion different from the Deficit Model:

| Feature | Deficit Model explanation | Alternative explanation |
| --- | --- | --- |
| Verb tenses: present tense form used for past tenses, such as 'I come home yesterday'. | Simplified grammar makes it difficult to express concept of time and could lead to misunderstandings. | In practice, this inflection is usually omitted only where an additional time marker ('yesterday') is included. What's more, there are other means of expressing time in Creole, such as 'Mary a go home', ('Mary is going home'), 'John en go home' ('John went home'). |
| Absence of verb 'to be' in sentences such as 'I a simple immigrant'. | Verb is omitted as part of simplification. | Verb is not really necessary in these contexts – and some languages other than English follow the Creole pattern in leaving it out (Russian, for instance). |
| Third person singular form of verb is not marked ('he go', not 'he goes'). | Loss of important grammatical distinction between the 'I' and 's/he' forms of a verb. | Standard English has also lost some distinctions in the past – for example, we no longer distinguish between 'you go' (singular) and 'you go' (plural). Many other languages do express this differently – so is a French speaker right to conclude that English is inferior to French because we do not use their distinction between 'tu' and 'vous'? Ironically, Creole does have a distinction between singular and plural 'you' ('yu' and 'unu'). |

## ACTIVITY 13

How did we come to have a number of non-standard and generally low-prestige dialectal varieties alongside the Standard version of English? In groups, try to agree which of these statements you think offers the best explanation of how such varieties have arisen:

1 Dialect speakers are simply making mistakes as a result of their faulty education, laziness or lack of intelligence.

2 Dialects are derived from, and therefore corrupted versions of, the standard, correct version of English that we started off with.

3 Other dialects of English have always existed alongside Standard English, but gradually lost respectability as Standard English became more important.

Compare your findings with the commentary on page 99.

# The origins of Standard English

Earlier, we considered the social and technological factors that made a 'standard' version of the language necessary (see Commentary 9 on page 98). However, if we retrace our historical steps to a time before electronic communications (the Internet, TV, telephones, radio), fast and convenient transport (aircraft, cars, railways), and widespread literacy with the availability of written texts, we arrive at a time when a standard was not really necessary.

Such a time was the fifteenth century – at least until a single technological invention signalled the beginning of the process that would eventually lead to the Standard English we take for granted today. That invention was, of course, the printing press, developed and introduced to England by William Caxton in the 1470s.

Until then, manuscripts were all handwritten and literacy was the preserve of a small privileged minority. In the two or three centuries after the invention of the press, books began to appear in unprecedented numbers, and we were on our way to becoming a print-based literate culture. However, for Caxton and the authors and printers who came after him, there was a problem: which dialect should they use?

## ACTIVITY 14 | C3.1A

Study the map, which shows the approximate linguistic geography of fifteenth-century England, together with its principal dialect divisions:

In the centuries after Caxton, the development of a print industry accelerated the pressures for a version of the language that could be recognised as a 'standard'. In groups, try to agree on which of the dialects indicated on the map you would back as the most likely candidate. As you make your judgement, consider the following factors:

• the centre of political power in England was London, where the monarch and the court were based

• the church – a very powerful institution during this vital period – was also based in London, though the Universities of Oxford and Cambridge were important seats of learning and centres for the training of priests, who would come from different parts of the kingdom to study there

- commercial printing was based in London

- there seems to have been considerable migration of people from the east and central Midlands to London during the fourteenth century

Now compare your suggestion with the commentary on page 99.

The outcome of this process of standardisation might have been very different if the distribution of power and influence had been otherwise. If, say, Newcastle upon Tyne had been the seat of government and the cathedral city of Durham exercised greater power than Oxford and Cambridge, this book might well have been written in the variety of English we now know as 'Geordie'.

However, such is the power now associated with Standard English that some people fear many of our regional dialects are in danger of disappearing (see page 40 in Module 1). Of course, English also enjoys tremendous power as a world language, a power once derived from the position of the British Empire but nowadays rooted in the economic and political power of the United States.

Here is a summary of the key points we examined concerning language and power:

- different varieties of language have different status (and power) in society

- these differences reflect the social, economic, political and cultural power of different groups

- many notions of 'correctness' and linguistic superiority are, in fact, the result of social influences

- some 'unofficial' varieties of language can enjoy covert prestige and can be used to express social identity

## The power of language

Another important aspect of our exploration of language and power is the power that resides in language itself. Language is not used simply to communicate information but also to persuade, convince, influence, inspire – and even intimidate. In this section we ask what makes a particular text powerful in any of these senses.

## ACTIVITY 15

We'll start by looking at a speech made by one the most influential politicians of the twentieth century, Nelson Mandela. Here is an extract from his inaugural address as President of South Africa, which he delivered to a huge crowd on 10 May 1994 (reproduced in B. McArthur (ed.), *The Penguin Book of Historic Speeches*).

Try to define those features of the speech that contribute to its power and impact on his listeners. Look in particular for any patterns (such as different kinds of repetition or contrast) Mandela uses to express and shape his ideas effectively. You may want to remind yourselves of the framework for stylistic analysis outlined in Module 1 (pages 11–13), and some of the linguistic terminology introduced there.

Finally, compare your analysis with the commentary on pages 99–100.

Today, all of us do, by our presence here, and by our celebrations in other parts of our country and the world, confer glory and hope to newborn liberty.

Out of the experience of an extraordinary human disaster that lasted too long, must be born a society of which all humanity will be proud.

Our daily deeds as ordinary South Africans must produce an actual South African reality that will reinforce humanity's belief in justice, strengthen its confidence in the nobility of the human soul and sustain all our hopes for a glorious life for all.

The time for the healing of the wounds has come. The moment to bridge the chasms that divide us has come. The time to build is upon us. We pledge ourselves to liberate all our people from the continuing bondage of poverty, deprivation, suffering, gender and other discrimination.

We are both humbled and elevated by the honour and privilege that you, the people of South Africa, have bestowed on us, as the first President of a united, democratic, non-racial and non-sexist South Africa, to lead our country out of the valley of darkness.

We understand it still that there is no easy road to freedom. We know it well that none of us acting alone can achieve success. We must therefore act together as a united people, for national reconciliation, for nation building, for the birth of a new world. Let there be justice for all. Let there be peace for all. Let there be work, bread, water and salt for all. Never, never and never again shall it be that this beautiful land will again experience the oppression of one by another and suffer the indignity of being the skunk of the world.

Let freedom reign. The sun shall never set on so glorious a human achievement! God bless Africa! Thank you.

Mandela's speech is a moving and apparently simple piece of public speaking, yet it conceals considerable artistry and linguistic control. It is an example of the art of powerful public speaking – oratory – and also illustrates many of the techniques widely used by speakers and writers seeking to exercise power over an audience of listeners or readers. The construction of language with the deliberate intention of producing this kind of impact is known as **rhetoric.**

You may find it helpful to refer to this summary of some common rhetorical techniques. They are listed here according to the categories in the stylistics framework.

**The power of language: some common techniques**

| Discourse structures | *problem–solution*: the speaker convinces the audience that they have a problem, then provides a solution *desire–need–fulfilment*: the speaker convinces the audience that there is something they need or desire, then promises they can have it if . . . |
| --- | --- |
| Sentence structures | *lists and repetition*: groups of three parallelism – repeating sentences with similar structures ('Let there be . . . Let there be . . . Let there be') contrasts and opposites rhetorical questions |
| Lexical choice | pronoun use direct address (second person: you) personal authority (first person singular: I) unity and bonding (first person plural: we) figurative language (metaphor, simile, personification) emotive language humorous language factual support and authority/citation of other authorities |
| Sounds and spellings | alliteration rhythmic slogans and repetitions |

In Module 3 you will find more examples of persuasive writing, together with suggestions for your own writing activities that will allow you to try putting some of these techniques into practice.

It is not only politicians and speech makers who use these techniques. That other great persuader, the advertising industry, exercises its power through language tailored to the products on sale, the targeted audience and the medium.

## ACTIVITY 16 — C3.1B

Gather a selection of your own advertisements for a variety of products, and choose one or two to analyse specifically in terms of their use of powerful or persuasive language. (Remember to check your analysis against the stylistics framework.) Make a presentation of your findings to the class.

Now look at the following advert for Colman's mustard, which appeared in the *Observer* Magazine in 1998. Write a full stylistic analysis of the text that explains how the advertisers use language to persuade readers to buy these products. Compare your analysis with the commentary on pages 100–101.

---

**The most exotic flavours traditionally come from the Far East.**

Norwich to be precise.

The explorers of old believed the earth to be flat and found treasures at the end of the rainbow.

It's the same today, at end of the A11.

In Norfolk, the earth's still flat and in the Colman's Mustard Shop in Norwich, where our speciality range of mustards is found, exotic treasures still await.

Here, from Hot Wholegrain through to Honey, are flavours that cut the mustard. And no wonder. Each one is the result of Colman's long experience in milling, blending and preparing mustards. Experience gained over a small matter of 180 years.

A visit to our Mustard Shop is a must.

Unless, of course, you visit the Colman's Mustard Shop in your local supermarket.

Undeniably, the East has its seedy side.

Whichever ones in the Mustard Shop range you try, be it as a condiment or recipe ingredient, you'll enjoy. That's an Eastern Promise.

For details of our speciality mustards please write to: The Colman's Mustard Shop, 3 Bridewell Alley, Norwich.

---

## Language and power in action: analysing conversation

Where are we most aware of the effects of differences of power, status and influence on our language? Probably in the countless everyday interactions between people across a range of domestic, professional, formal and informal contexts. In other words, we need to look closely at conversation and how it works.

Talking to each other seems so natural to us that we could easily assume that conversation is a random, unstructured business. However, we have already seen (Module 1, pages 33–35) that different kinds of conversations follow different patterns, and that what we can say in different situations is limited by context, purpose and audience.

## Your turn or mine?

Perhaps the most obvious structural feature of everyday speech is that we usually take turns to talk. Of course, there are occasions when someone interrupts, or is cut short, or starts to talk at the same time as someone else, but on the whole talking is a fairly orderly business. Even when disagreement is being expressed and tempers are frayed, we tend to observe this basic rule of human conversation: turn-taking.

The most basic unit of conversation is the **adjacency pair**. This is when one utterance – 'Have you been drinking?' – is immediately followed by an appropriate response – 'Certainly not, officer'. To some extent, the first utterance limits the kinds of possible response. The question 'Have you been drinking?' could be followed by a denial (as above) or a confession – 'Yes, I'm afraid I have' – or even a counter-question or accusation – 'What makes you say that?' Other responses are possible, but these are unlikely or potentially provocative – 'What if I have?' (challenge); 'Get lost!' (insult/command) – or just impossible or insane – 'Yellow', 'One hundred and sixty', or 'That's my hamster'.

## ACTIVITY 17

For each of the following openings, suggest the kinds of response that are most likely to complete the adjacency pair. The first one is provided as an example:

| Opening | Possible responses |
|---|---|
| 'That's a nice top' (observation) | 'Thanks!' (acknowledgement)<br>'I got it in the sales' (information)<br>'Yes it is, isn't it?' (agreement)<br>'Do you think so?' (disagreement) |
| 'Can I have a word?' | |
| 'Can I help you?' | |
| 'Leave me alone' | |
| 'How do you plead? Guilty, or not guilty?' | |

Of course, most conversations consist of many adjacency pairs in which the response to one pair becomes the start of the next:

'How are you?'
'Fine thanks. And you?'
'Been better . . .'

In extended talk, we move from turn to turn with little conscious effort – but we take our cues to speak from a number of clues provided by the current speaker. We then take our turn – or 'seize the floor' – until the next person's turn.

In a classroom this mechanism is obvious; teachers may expect pupils to wait for a question, or to request a turn by putting up their hand. In less structured talk, however, the cues may be less clear.

## ACTIVITY 18

In groups, try to identify the types of cue that enable us to seize the floor. Think about:

- visual cues (does a speaker give us a sign?)

- phonetic cues (does something happen to the speaker's voice?)

- syntactic clues (can we tell from a speaker's sentences when she or he is coming to an end?)

Compare your suggestions with those in the commentary on page 101.

As well as recognising when we can take a turn, we must also choose what kind of thing it is appropriate to say at any given time. Could there be underlying 'rules' that help us string our exchanges into what we recognise as conversation?

The linguist H. P. Grice tried to define the various rules, or maxims, that control how we respond to each other and construct conversations by moving from turn to turn. He maintained that when a conversation is working normally, we tend to assume that:

- what we say will have something to do with what has just been said (the maxim of relevance)

- what we say will be neither too long nor too short (the maxim of quantity)

- what we say is likely to be true (the maxim of quality)

- what we say is likely to be clear and meaningful (the maxim of manner)

Of course, these maxims can be broken, and often are – people lie or ramble on, people can be unco-operative, unclear or obscure. But when this happens, according to Grice, we become aware that there is something 'abnormal' about the conversation.

The way these maxims work in practice is likely to vary according to social contexts and relationships. One way of understanding how we negotiate these relationships is to think of everything we say as having both a surface meaning and a social function. Take this simple exchange:

A: How are you doing?
B: Not bad thanks. Yourself?
A: Ay, not bad. Bit nippy out, though.

The meaning of A's first turn, or utterance, is clear enough — it seems to be an enquiry about B's health or wellbeing. However, in many situations — and this was actually overheard in a corner shop where B regularly stopped to buy sweets and newspapers — the social function of the utterance is to establish a pleasant, social relationship and to create an opportunity for some informal interaction. B's reply similarly has a meaning and a function; the meaning is vague and non-committal (something like 'I'm OK'), but at least by replying appropriately B signals a willingness to develop the relationship. If B had stopped with 'Not bad, thanks', leaving A to ask the next question, the function might have been to suggest: 'I'm happy to respond to your friendliness and I'm not going to be rude, but I have no particular wish to converse as I'm in a bit of a hurry'. However, the 'Yourself?' that B adds has the effect of putting the ball back in A's court, equalising the conversation in terms of the willingness to participate.

This kind of small talk is sometimes called **phatic talk**; its function is mainly social rather than about carrying out a particular transaction. In many informal and social situations much of a conversation may be phatic, but in other situations this may not be the case.

## ACTIVITY 19

Think of a typical visit to a GP's surgery. If the doctor greets you with the words 'How are you?', how might the meaning and function of this question differ from the casual enquiry of the corner shopkeeper?

Now consider another familiar situation, in which the conversation goes something like this:

A: I was just wondering if you fancied coming over tonight (.) you know (.) for a drink and that
B: (3) Well . . . I'd like to but (.) I've really got to stay in tonight (.) I've got that history essay to hand in tomorrow

A's meaning and function are both reasonably clear. His meaning is 'Do you want to come over?', and the function is to explore the extent to which B is interested in him. Suggest why A does not simply *say* 'Do you want to come over?', or even 'Do you fancy me?'

B's reply is very revealing. The meaning is clear: the answer is 'no', and for a good reason. What do you think is the function of the pauses, the hesitant 'well', and the excuse offered?

Compare your interpretation with the commentary on page 101.

We often discover that running beneath the surface of our conversations is a whole set of functions and intentions that may be quite different from the surface meanings of our utterances. In drama and theatre, actors call this aspect of conversation the subtext; in linguistics, the study of these underlying meanings and social functions is called pragmatics.

## ACTIVITY 20

The classroom is a good place in which to start to examine the pragmatics of everyday dialogue. In most schools, the conversations that take place in classrooms follow clearly defined patterns, and reflect the purpose of the interaction (education/instruction), the context (pupils in a class with a teacher) and power relationships (the teacher has more power than the students).

As you examine the following transcript of conversations from a maths class, try to define the 'rules' of this interaction by considering:

- who leads, or dominates the conversation, and how we can tell
- who asks the questions, and what kinds of questions they are
- what the teacher does with the responses
- how the topic (what gets talked about) is controlled
- what you notice about any interruptions or overlaps
- other ways in which the teacher exercises power in the conversation
- what social functions (as opposed to surface meanings) any of the utterances may have

Now compare your analysis with the commentary on page 102.

| | |
|---|---|
| Teacher: | First of all (.) how do you think we can get T (.) from that (.) concluded situation (.) |
| Pupil(s): | (inaudible) |
| T: | Sorry (.) no (.) somebody say something |
| P: | (.) Hooke's law |
| T: | Hooke's law is gonna be one yeah (.) how (.) what what will be the unknowns in that (.) we don't know the lambda (.) do we know the natural length |
| P: | Yes |
| T: | Yes (.) do we know the extension |
| P: | (2) Yes |
| T: | Why |
| P: | Because you've got that nought point zero seven (.) so you can do it if you divide by that (.) |
| T: | Right (.) well done (.) you've got 24 centimetres on (.) on either side (.) so you can get the extension (3) any questions so far (.) good (.) let's move on (.) |

In a classroom, the powerful position of the teacher is reflected in the unique set of rules that seem to control the kinds of conversations taking place. In other social contexts, differences in the status of participants may also be reflected in the underlying 'rules of play'.

## ACTIVITY 21

Consider a typical family conversation round the meal table. Try to suggest how the status/power of a family member is reflected in the amount of talking they are permitted to do before being interrupted or told to be quiet.

## ACTIVITY 22

In many social contexts, the right to ask questions and expect truthful answers is an indicator of power. Suggest some examples.

In the following two situations, the respondents' refusal to answer a question to which they know the answer is potentially provocative. Suggest why, referring to Grice's maxims as appropriate:

(1)  Teacher:      'What's your name?'
     Pupil:        'Why?'

(2)  Policeman:    'What's your name?'
     Young man:    'Mickey Mouse.'

The right to judge other people's utterances is another sign of power or status. If you ask a stranger for directions, listen encouragingly, and then respond with 'Very clear directions. Well done!', you may provoke an unlooked-for reaction. Suggest why.

In school, at work or in our dealings with authority, the different degrees of power people possess may be obvious, but in social and other informal situations we may feel that we are all equals. However, even among people of apparently equal social status, it is likely that some are 'more equal than others'. Conversational patterns are affected not only by differences of social status and power, but also by differences in the personal status of participants.

## ACTIVITY 23

To explore this idea, let's look at a conversation recorded during an evening meal at a house where a group of middle-aged friends have gathered. Use the framework of questions introduced on pages 34–5 to analyse the conversational relationship of participants A and B:

A:  This head (.)
B:  Oh (2)
A:  Heads have to be able to understand (.)// the kids that they're dealing with
B:  //mm
A:  don't they (.)
B:  Yeah
A:  I mean if they're going to do a good job they have to be able to understand the background (.) the problems that the kids they're dealing with have got and //

B: // yeah

A: and (2) being (2) prejudging this bloke // it seems

B: // well that's all we can do because he didn't give anything of himself did he

A: (.) he didn't (3) it wasn't (I) I think what they should have done that day before was they should what they did with the em when the candidates came in for the em (I)

B: // deputy's job

A: // yeah they should have they should have had a programme of people for them to talk to

B: Mm absolutely

Now compare your analysis with the commentary on page 102.

The conversation in Activity 23 shows two speakers co-operating to produce talk, even though one speaker (B) settles for a secondary and supportive role. What happens, though, where there is potential conflict and disagreement between speakers?

## ACTIVITY 24

Examine the following transcript of a workplace conversation between a manager (A) and an employee (B). As you analyse the conversation, consider especially:

- where in the conversation you can see evidence of tension between the two speakers

- how the higher status and extra power of A are reflected

- whether A does anything to make the situation less severe or confrontational

Now compare your analysis with the commentary on page 103.

(A's office. B knocks and enters)

A: Ah (2) Brian

B: (2) Mr Howden (.) you said you // wanted to see me

A: // yes yes do come in and take a seat

B: Thanks

A: (.) Thank you for er (.) sparing me a few moments

B: (.) Well it sounded as if (.) it sounded rather serious (.) is there (.) is there a problem

A: Yes I'm afraid so

B: (3) oh (.)

A: You'll remember Brian that we spoke last week about the complaint we'd received

B: Yes (.) // and I'd like

A: // and we agreed I think that you'd try to pacify the situation as soon as possible

B: Yeah

A: Well I'm afraid I received a telephone call this morning from David Harrison and I have to say that he is not a happy bunny

B: (2) Oh I see (.) perhaps I could just explain what // happened after I saw you

A: // in fact from what he said the situation seems to have deteriorated somewhat // and it does seem that we need to do some work to start

B: // mm

A: putting things straight

# Analysing talk: summary

When examining conversational data, you may want to use a systematic framework that reminds you of the different questions to ask at different linguistic levels. This approach will also help you to achieve one of the Assessment Objectives: to 'know and use key features of frameworks for the systematic study of spoken and written English':

## Conversation: applying an analytical framework

| Element | Key question | Techniques and strategies |
|---------|-------------|--------------------------|
| Pragmatic framework | How does the dialogue reflect social relationships and implied meanings? | Discuss this in terms of turn-taking patterns, agenda and topic management, speakers' forms of address to each other, politeness strategies, phatic talk and implied meaning. Focus especially on the social function of utterances rather than just the surface meaning. |
| Grammatical framework | What grammatical structures does each speaker use, and with what effects? | Discuss this in terms of sentence types, lengths and structures; use of Standard English or non-standard features; non-fluency features such as slips, false starts and repetitions. |
| Semantic framework | What kinds of meaning does each speaker contribute? | Discuss this in terms of the most frequent utterance type of each speaker – a question, a command, a joke, a confession, etc. |
| Lexical framework | What kinds of vocabulary does each speaker use? | Discuss this in terms of register; degrees of formality, colloquiality, topic specificity; factual or emotional content; personal or impersonal style; literal or figurative expressions; status and discourse. |
| Phonetic/ phonological framework | What are the vocal characteristics of speakers and what are the effects of those characteristics? | If information is available, discuss this aspect in terms of intonation, stress, tempo, rhythm and pauses. |

# Language and gender

In recent years there has been a great deal of interest in the relationship between gender and language use. This reflects a more general concern with the changing roles of men and women in society, and the social trends of the last 30 years or so whereby many traditional assumptions about gender roles have been challenged.

There are two main issues implied in an investigation of language and gender:

- the vocabulary that is used to refer to men and women

- the differences in the ways men and women actually use language themselves

## Sugar and spice and puppy dogs' tails: talking of gender

> Sugar and spice and all things nice,
> That's what little girls are made of.
> Slugs and snails and puppy dogs' tails,
> That's what little boys are made of.

It is clear from the way we use English that we think gender is significant. When we refer to people for whatever reason, we will often specify the gender of the person concerned even when it is not particularly relevant. We talk about a 'boy' or a 'girl' more often than just a 'child', a 'father' or 'mother' more often than a 'parent', and 'brother' or 'sister' rather than 'sibling'. There is no word in English for aunt or uncle that is not gender specific, and the overwhelming majority of first names immediately identify their bearer's gender.

If we routinely represent people in terms of their gender, are there any differences in the ways males and females are referred to? We don't need to think very long before coming up with the answer.

Let's start by looking at the titles that we give or are given when identifying ourselves. Unless we have an inherited or other special title, there are two traditional alternatives for men and two for women. If we are male, we have the choice of either Mr or Master. If we are female, we might be Mrs or Miss. On the face of it, these two pairs of titles look as if they are opposites of each other – Mr/Mrs and Miss/Master. In fact their use and meanings are very different.

## ACTIVITY 25
C3.1A

*Same difference?* Define the differences between the uses and meanings of 'Master' and 'Miss'.

Also, explain the differences between the titles available to adult men and women, and suggest what these differences reveal about different attitudes towards men and women.

What reasons do you think 1960s feminist groups may have given for popularising the term 'Ms'? Describe your attitudes towards its use.

*Sticks and stones.* Brainstorm a list of the terms of abuse most commonly used about people of either gender. Sum up the differences you find, and try to account for them.

*What's my line?* The following titles or jobs are listed in male/female pairs. For each pair, decide whether the terms are true equivalents, and describe any differences between them: manager/manageress, father/mother, author/authoress, Lord/Lady, master/mistress.

Now compare all your responses with the commentary on pages 103–104.

## Gender and semantics: marked and unmarked categories

As we have just seen, one feature of our English vocabulary is a tendency for the female form of a title to be more obviously 'marked' than the male form. This can often reflect a particular 'mindset', in which we assume that certain roles or occupations are inevitably assigned to a particular gender.

### ACTIVITY 26

The following extract from a careers bulletin mentions a number of professional people. Students were asked to supply the missing words indicated by the numbered dashes in the text.

Which pronouns do you think English students are likely to suggest, and what do you think these choices reveal about language and gender? Compare your answers with the commentary on page 105.

Next week as part of our Careers programme a number of specialist professionals will be visiting the college. An engineer will talk about careers in the mechanical and electrical engineering industries. (1) — will meet any interested students in Room 12.

A nurse will also be available to discuss career routes into Nursing, and (2) — will be in Room 20. Meanwhile Dr Hibbert from the Cambridge Road Medical Practice will speak to potential medical students in Room 14 where (3) — will also show a video entitled 'Careers in Medicine'.

## One small step: generic man

One example of our gender-related use of language is the word 'man' itself. When Neil Armstrong stepped onto the Moon in 1969 he delivered a carefully scripted epigram. In fact, he slightly misquoted the lines and should have said 'That's one small step for a man, one giant leap for mankind'.

Armstrong omitted the 'a', saying instead 'That's one small step for man . . .'. The 'correct' version uses two different senses of the idea 'man'. Had he used this version, Armstrong would have referred to himself as 'a man'. This can mean both (1) an adult male and (2) a member of the human species (as in 'man evolved from apes'). We can call this second meaning of the term the generic use. But which meaning did Armstrong actually intend? In the event of the first person to land being female, would we have referred to her the first as 'woman' on the moon, and would she have said, 'That's one small step for a woman . . .'? Of course, the epigram works by contrasting the first reference to 'man' with the unmistakably generic 'mankind'. However, in the version that Armstrong actually spoke, 'man' without the 'a' sounds as if it is generic too, thus lessening the effectiveness of the saying.

This illustrates a problem with 'man'. It is ambiguous, being used as both a generic and a gender-specific term. In practice, this can lead to problems: it is quite possible to say 'all men [generic] should live in peace' and include women; but we can hardly say 'the man [generic] next door has just become a mother'! In the second example, where a specific person is identified, the word must refer to gender.

Some people object to the generic use of 'man' because it ignores or devalues the role of women. So should we actually change our use of English to reflect modern ideas about gender roles and equality of opportunity?

## ACTIVITY 27                                                      C3.1A

The table lists several examples of commonly used expressions involving the generic 'man'. Add any more you can think of, then provide reasoned objections to the use of the term as it stands. In the third column, suggest an alternative that is free of any gender reference. Compare your notes with the commentary on page 105.

| Extract | Objection | Alternative term |
| --- | --- | --- |
| The chairman is expected to address the shareholders this morning. | | |
| Sam the fireman put on his shiny new helmet. | | |
| Report to the site foreman at 9.00 am. | | |
| There's a new postman on our route. | | |
| We'll have to reduce manning levels in every department. | | |
| | | |
| | | |
| | | |

## Gender in discourse

The second part of our investigation concerns the ways in which men and women actually use language themselves. The questions that researchers have been asking over the last 20 years or so include:

- Are there differences between the use of non-standard accents and dialects among men and women?

- Do men and women use different vocabularies?

- Do men and women behave differently in conversational contexts?

- What are the explanations for, and implications of, these differences?

### *Gender and accent*

Earlier in this module, we saw how researchers have explored the relationship between the use of non-standard accent and dialect features and the social class of speakers (see pages 62–9). In particular, we saw how sociolinguists like William Labov in the USA and Peter Trudgill in the UK focused on specific aspects of a region's speech to define precisely this relationship among a sample of speakers. Both researchers were also interested in the issue of gender, and reported some significant differences between male and female speech in their findings.

### ACTIVITY 28

From your own experience and observation, what difference, if any, would you expect to find between men and women of a similar social class in their use of regional speech? Think in terms of the 'strength' of accents and the use of non-standard dialectal grammar.

Now compare these anecdotal expectations with the following data from Trudgill's Norwich accent research.

Trudgill's study measured the number of speakers in each social class who used the form 'runnin' rather than 'running', etc. in the speech samples he recorded. The table shows these as percentages in each class for male and female speakers:

| Runnin', talkin', washin' . . . | | | | | |
|---|---|---|---|---|---|
| | Middle class | Lower middle class | Upper working class | Middle working class | Lower working class |
| Males | 4 | 27 | 81 | 91 | 100 |
| Females | 0 | 3 | 68 | 81 | 97 |

## ACTIVITY 29

Write down any conclusions that can reasonably be inferred from this data about differences between male and female speech. Remember to be cautious: the data is based on a limited sample, and some researchers have questioned the way in which Trudgill allocated female speakers to different social classes.

Compare these findings with the expectations you discussed in Activity 28, and suggest possible explanations for the apparent trend revealed by the data. Finally, compare your responses with the commentary on pages 105–106.

## *Gender and dialect*

Other studies have set out to test the proposition that women are less likely to use forms of dialectal grammar than men of the same social class and are therefore more likely to adopt the grammatical structures of Standard English. In 1982, the researcher Jenny Cheshire set out to find some answers by investigating the speech of some young speakers in Reading. Her findings are shown in the table.

**Use of non-standard grammar by adolescent boys and girls in Reading**

| Example of non-standard form used | Boys | Girls |
|---|---|---|
| 'I don't want nothing' (double negative) | 100 | 75 |
| 'That ain't working' (non-standard negative 'to be') | 74 | 42 |
| 'That's what I does' (non-standard first person 'do') | 71 | 50 |

## ACTIVITY 30                                    C3.3, N3.1

Examine Cheshire's data carefully. Note down any conclusions that can reasonably be drawn from her findings, and suggest possible explanations for the apparent trend that they reveal. Compare your notes with the commentary on page 106.

## *Gender and conversation*

When we examined conversation earlier in this module, we found that the status, power and influence of speakers are reflected in the way people interact and converse. As women have traditionally been associated with less powerful positions in society, and are stereotypically associated with subordinate roles, could it be that men and women actually behave differently in conversation?

One particularly influential study set out to discover if this is the case. In 1975, the researchers Zimmerman and West published an account of their study based at the University of California. They taped conversations between pairs of men and women and examined the way they took turns in same-sex and mixed conversations. They noted the frequency with which speakers of each gender overlapped (started speaking just before the previous one had finished) or interrupted (cut off the previous speaker, preventing him/her from finishing).

The findings of Zimmerman and West (1975) can be summarised as follows:

- *Same sex*: in 20 conversations, there were 22 overlaps and 7 interruptions

- *Mixed sex*: in 11 conversations, there were 9 overlaps by men and 0 by women, and 46 interruptions by men and 2 by women

## ACTIVITY 31

Write down any conclusions you think can be drawn from these findings. Also note down your reactions: are you surprised or alarmed, for example? Offer some explanations for the differences in behaviour that these findings seem to reveal.

Compare your notes with the analysis offered by Jennifer Coates in *Men, Women and Language*, as quoted in the commentary on page 106.

## Men and women: talking the same language?

Not only do men and women behave differently when it comes to turn-taking, they also differ in many other significant aspects of conversational behaviour. This, at least, was the conclusion of writers such as Dale Spender and Robin Lakoff in the 1970s, and much subsequent research has confirmed many of their findings, as summarised here below.

## Gender and conversation: a summary of research findings

- Women use more questions than men, and often do so in a phatic way to keep conversations going, rather than simply to obtain information. Men are more likely to see questions as requests for information, and are less likely to use them just to maintain the conversation

- Men are more likely to disregard Grice's 'maxim of relevance', and to insist on their point even if it involves a change of subject and is unconnected to what has gone before

- Men are more likely to compete for the floor, and arguments in all male groups may include more aggressive uses of language (such as insults, raised voices, threats)

- Women tend to listen more actively and supportively, making more use of minimal responses during another speaker's turn to indicate interest and agreement. Men may delay their minimal responses and thus convey impatience or lack of interest

- Women tend to be more tentative, using more frequent hedges (see Commentary 24 on page 103) and **question tags** (as in 'We could do that, couldn't we?')

- In general, women tend towards co-operation; men towards competition

---

**ACTIVITY 32**                                                    **C3.3, N3.3**

It is time to try out some of these ideas by examining your own data. Arrange to make a recording of either a mixed-sex conversation or two similar conversations involving only males or only females. These may be taken from the broadcast media or, preferably, a live conversation. (If you tape live speech, remember always to follow the guidelines given on page 9 of Module 1.)

Transcribe a section of the tape, making sure you indicate where interruptions or overlapping occur. Examine the data closely to test the general findings discussed above. This will mean:

- counting and comparing examples of interruptions/overlaps, questions, minimal responses, hedges and question tags

- commenting closely on these examples

- applying our conversational analysis framework (see page 83)

- presenting your findings in a report

## Language and occupational groups

The third major social context for language use that we identified at the beginning of this module was occupation. This refers to the context and circumstances in which we use language to carry out our daily work. The occupational groups to which people belong can shape and influence their uses of language in two principal ways.

Firstly, a shared language, code or jargon within a profession or trade may act as a kind of shorthand to help members exchange specialised information quickly, and also as a kind of linguistic glue bonding members of that group together.

Secondly, the way members of a particular profession use language can reflect their power and status in society, and express their particular values and interests.

So far in this module, we have examined examples of the language of a politician (Nelson Mandela, page 74), and the advertising industry (Colman's Mustard, page 76). Here, we consider how these aspects are illustrated in the case of two occupational groups: teachers and vets.

### Occupational group 1: teachers and school reports

How might the language of teachers illustrate the two aspects of occupational language suggested above? Firstly, they may share a subject-specific vocabulary related to their teaching subjects and the world of education in general. Secondly, the way teachers speak and write is likely to reveal both their power and influence – through judgements of their students' work and behaviour, for example – and their values. For most teachers, concepts like 'progress', 'hard work', 'child development' and 'good behaviour' are important and desirable; 'laziness' and 'cheek' are not.

We have already discovered (when examining conversation) that teachers' conversational behaviour – at least in the classroom – is unusual. Part of that behaviour involves asking questions the answers to which they already know, and evaluating the quality of the responses they receive from their students. We'll turn now to another sample of teacher-speak – a collection of school reports.

## ACTIVITY 33

Study the selection of reports printed below. For each of them, ask: (1) Has the writer used any subject-specific lexis? (2) How has the writer expressed his/her authority and judgements? (3) How does the language of the reports express the key values of this occupation?

Compare your analysis with the commentary on pages 106–107.

### REPORT 1: GARY, FRENCH

Gary has made limited progress. His grasp of verb constructions is very weak and this has prevented him from improving his position.

### REPORT 2: GARY, ECONOMICS

Some of Gary's class work has reached a reasonable standard, but his examination performance was very weak indeed. As yet he lacks knowledge of basic economic concepts, and intensive revision is needed if he is to have any chance in the final examination.

### REPORT 3: JOHN, MATHS

John has shown that he has the ability to succeed with this GCSE mathematics course. If he has not defeated the examiners in November we can be confident of his doing so in June.

### REPORT 4: DAVID, CHEMISTRY

The examination showed what I suspected – that David doesn't actually know much Chemistry. He must get beyond the feeling that if he can just follow the work in class then all will be well. At a superficial level he is very co-operative and enthusiastic, but he is also extremely complacent. If there are topics where lack of background is causing problems he must do something about it, and ask for help.

## REPORT 5: JENNY, ENGLISH

Jenny continues to find the course challenging, but should be able to achieve some success in the examination provided she increases her work rate. She ought to seek help when in doubt, and she must ensure that all assignments are handed in on time.

## Occupational group 2: vets

Vets, like other professionals involved in a highly specialised field, have developed a technical language that enables them to exchange information about animals, their diseases and appropriate medication in an efficient manner. As in other professions, specialist publications written by and for experts in the field offer professionals the opportunity to talk to each other in the language they understand.

One such publication is the *Veterinary Record*. It contains articles about animal welfare, new treatments and medicines, but also offers advertisers the chance to market products aimed at this specialist audience. In such adverts we can expect to see a mixture of the register associated with the occupational group and the characteristic strategies and techniques of an advert. Here's an advertisement for a treatment for an ear condition that appeared in the *Veterinary Record* on 30 October 1999.

---

# OTOMAX: 0–93% in 7 days!

93% of otitis externa cases treated with OTOMAX turned in a good or excellent response in just 7 days.

When it comes to beating this condition, this new marque from Schering-Plough Animal Health really has it all.

Thanks to its unique hydrocarbon gel technology, OTOMAX goes round even the tightest bend and really does stick to the aural canal. Vets, owners and pets will love the way it handles.

When you open it up, there's an impressive 3-way combination of clotrimazole, betamethasone and gentamicin.

Once you've test-driven OTOMAX, you won't want to use anything else.

---

## ACTIVITY 34                                                   C3.3

Read the Otomax advert carefully, then use the stylistics framework on pages 11–12 to examine the ways in which it uses language to promote the product. Consider in particular:

- how the advertiser exploits the audience's familiarity with the clichés of car advertising

- how the advert uses rhetorical devices

- how the lexis helps identify the target audience, its interests and its values

Compare your analysis with the commentary on page 107.

# Preparing for the examination

## The examination

The examination for this module of the AQA Specification A lasts 2 hours. In that time you have to:

- study a selection of short spoken and written extracts illustrating aspects of the topics Language and Power, Language and Gender, Language and Occupational Groups

- answer two questions based on these texts, dividing your time equally between them

In your answers you must:

- demonstrate your skills of linguistic analysis

- apply what you have learned about language in social contexts to the texts on the paper

- relate the texts on the paper to the wider linguistic issues studied in this module

## Preparing to meet the Assessment Objectives

It is important that your answers meet the relevant Assessment Objectives for this module (see page 57). As you approach the examination, you need to gear your revision of this module to meeting them in full:

| Assessment Objective | This means you need to ... | Revision tip |
|---|---|---|
| 'communicate clearly the knowledge, understanding and insight appropriate to the study of language, using appropriate terminology and accurate and coherent written expression' | . . . write precisely and in some detail about power, gender and occupational groups, as revealed in the texts, using appropriate linguistic terminology. Write in accurate, clear English, and organise and express your analysis coherently. | Review your personal glossary and the one printed at the end of this book. Make sure you understand and can use the new linguistic terms you have learned. |

| | | |
|---|---|---|
| 'know and use key features of frameworks for the systematic study of spoken and written English' | . . . apply a relevant analytical framework to the texts. Be systematic in your approach to the analysis. | Review the different levels of linguistic analysis: discourse structure, form, sentence and grammar, lexis, and sounds and spelling. Revise the stylistics and analysing talk frameworks, and the list of persuasive features, and test your analytical skills by applying them to texts you find for yourself. |
| 'understand, discuss and explore concepts and issues relating to language in use' | . . . show how power, gender and occupational context influence the way language is used in the texts you are given. | Revise each area thoroughly; don't gamble by trying to preselect the ones you would like to focus on. Memorise the main findings of the research studies by Labov, Trudgill and Cheshire. |
| 'distinguish, describe and interpret variation in the meanings and forms of spoken and written language according to context' | . . . offer a detailed interpretation of how meanings are conveyed in the texts you analyse. Explain how the social contexts of these texts (in terms of power, gender or occupation) have helped shape their form and meanings. | Review your own analytical exercises and the samples provided in the commentaries. |

## In the exam . . .

You will be asked to analyse individual texts, but also to show that you can bring to your analysis a wider knowledge and experience of linguistic matters. Don't simply write an essay about everything you know – but do look for opportunities to relate features you find in the given texts to relevant things you studied in the module.

# Commentaries

## Activity 1

Charlotte is fairly typical of many people these days, in that she has moved both geographically (from Manchester to Birmingham and now London) and socially (her parents had occupations that might traditionally be regarded as working class, but she is now in a professional, middle class occupation). Her correspondingly wide language repertoire makes her a particularly interesting linguistic subject.

The issues that you discussed may have included:

- How much of a Manchester accent did she grow up with, and does she still have it? Will she have lost it at university or afterwards? What might have caused her to do so – or not?

- In formal management meetings at work, would she adopt rather formal language styles and an accent closer to RP? As a manager, what sort of language does she use to give instructions and exert her authority? Does she use terminology or jargon that is specific to her company?

- What happens when she meets up again with her parents or friends from the North? Perhaps her original accent resurfaces as she re-establishes her bond with her school friends. Does the same thing happen when she visits her parents? How would they react if she spoke to them at home the same way she speaks to her colleagues at work?

- No doubt Charlotte's language at home is different again; as a mother, she uses language to convey affection, encouragement and authority, as needs arise, and to discuss family issues with her husband and the children.

## Activity 2

You probably identified this as a call in which a customer (C) is making a complaint to a customer service adviser (A) at a call centre. The nature of the call, and the occupation of the customer adviser, defines each speaker's role. The customer expects a response to his concerns, whereas the role of the adviser is to represent the company and do what he can to satisfy the customer. The conversation is not personal, but purely about a commercial or professional transaction.

In terms of status, the relationship is clearly an unequal one – the adviser addresses the caller politely, as 'Mr Brown' and 'sir', while identifying himself as Adam. To the customer, the adviser uses polite expressions such as 'How may I help you?', whereas the customer is bluntly casual ('I'm getting a bit fed up') and even resorts to sarcasm ('name, number and shoe size'). The adviser skilfully combines his requests for information with expressions of concern ('I'm very sorry') and assurance ('I'm sure I'll be able to sort // things out') to calm the customer's irritation, and he makes sympathetic noises as the customer starts to explain the problem ('mm', 'Oh'). The adviser only speaks when it is clearly his turn, whereas at the end of the extract the customer cuts in and interrupts him.

Advisers are trained to handle calls like this in a particular way – whatever they might personally feel about the caller, they have to enact a particular role and use language in the ways required by their employers.

## Activity 4

*Powerful individuals.* It would be surprising if you hadn't at least considered the Prime Minister and perhaps the Chancellor of the Exchequer as powerful individuals. You may have thought about the Queen, and then thought again – how much power does she actually have these days? On the other hand, media giants such as Rupert Murdoch (owner of Sky and News International, which controls *The Times*, the *Sun* and the *News of the World*) clearly have tremendous influence, as does someone like Bill Gates, the owner of Microsoft. You may also have decided that individual scientists and artists exercise considerable power too, though the influence of some of these (such as pop groups like the Spice Girls or Oasis) may be rather short-lived.

*Powerful groups.* The answers to these questions may seem obvious. People from non-white backgrounds are generally under-represented in professions where power and influence are to be found (politics, the law, business management, the media), as are women, despite some advances in their position in the last 30 years. On the face of it, the people who control large businesses (managers, directors) would seem to have more power than those who work in them, and people who work in key positions in the media may have more influence than those who merely consume their products. In the North/South debate, northerners often complain that people closest to the southern centres of political and economic power enjoy greater wealth and influence.

## Activity 6

While it may be true that most newsreaders are university educated, it is unlikely that they all grew up speaking RP. The presenter and former newsreader Sue Lawley, for example, reports making a conscious decision to change her native Birmingham accent whilst at university at Oxford. So the 'schools' explanation is likely to be the least significant one.

The 'understanding' explanation seems more attractive: after all, RP is widely used and understood, and is associated with clarity of delivery. However, programmes such as *EastEnders* and *Coronation Street* regularly top the popularity ratings, and even the weather reports that precede or follow news bulletins are often delivered by speakers with regional accents. Does this mean that we spend our time watching soap operas and weather forecasts that we can barely understand?

No; rather, as Giles's study suggests, it is because RP is associated in our culture with intelligence, authority and education. We are more likely to believe that the news is truthful and to be taken seriously if it is delivered in RP than if it were spoken in, say, a Liverpudlian accent. Ultimately, this is linked to the stereotypes commonly associated with people from different regions and different social backgrounds. The weather is a different matter, as it is less 'serious' than the news, and soap operas are, of course, fictional.

## Activity 7

Trudgill's figures confirm that there is a clear, if quite complicated, relationship between accent and social class. The *n* for *ng* sound and the glottal stop '*t*' are very widely used by working class speakers, whereas many of these may not use the 'missing h' feature. In all cases, though, middle class speakers are much less likely to include these non-RP features in their speech, with the 'missing h' very rare. Could it be that 'dropping your aitches' is often seen as a sign of 'poor' or 'lazy' speech, and is thus avoided by the status conscious?

This raises interesting questions about what happens to the accents of people who are socially mobile, and who feel somewhat self-conscious about their working class regional speech – like some of the northern businessmen quoted in the 'North Mouth Divide' article on page 63.

## Activity 8

There may be good reasons for suggesting all three options. The visitors' accent enjoys overt prestige, and young people may well feel attracted to the lifestyle and values it represents – the city with all its excitement, sophistication and affluence, which they do not currently enjoy. Alternatively, if the contact between the two groups of people was very limited, it may well be that there was no real opportunity for much 'cross-pollination' to take place. The third option may occur if the locals felt some resentment towards the outsiders and felt the need to strengthen their sense of identity in the face of such an invasion.

In fact, Labov found that the young men on the island were moving away from the prestige pronunciation and thus resisting the apparent power and overt prestige of the linguistic forms of the wealthy.

Labov's study illustrates some important aspects of the relationship between regional varieties and power. Sometimes an apparently low prestige form can enjoy a different sort of prestige within the community of people who speak it. This hidden strength of regional forms is sometimes called **covert prestige**.

The study also shows that whole communities, as well as individuals, can shift their speech according to whether or not they wish to be accepted as part of another group – in which case their speech may grow closer to the group's, a process called **convergence**. On the other hand, as in Martha's Vineyard, the opposite may occur: to signal our wish not to be identified with people we dislike we may move away from them, a process known as **divergence**.

## Activity 9

Among the many possible reasons, perhaps you included these:

- mass media (TV, press) are produced for national and international consumption

- printed texts have to be written for universal understanding and consumption – it would be impractical to produce different versions of the same books in different dialects

- electronic communications reach not just across the UK but (via the Internet) the world

- we now belong to a very mobile community of English speakers: many of us travel frequently for business and pleasure

- English is a world language and foreign learners need to have one version to learn

## Activity 10

Perhaps you suggested that it was important to the children to use the language of their friends and fit in with them, rather than use the Standard forms. If so, this should remind you of the Martha's Vineyard study (see page 66) and the covert prestige of non-standard forms.

Turning to the second question, children need to be able to use Standard English to gain qualifications and function effectively in a print-orientated society. Even in speech, non-standard English is often seen as 'poor' or 'incorrect' and may present an unfavourable impression if used in formal or professional contexts. The counter-argument is that children can understand the need to use Standard English when necessary, but should not be discouraged from using regional speech in informal contexts where it is perfectly acceptable. Besides, it is impossible for schools to tell children how to speak in the playground or among friends.

## Activity 11

A similar pattern to the accents study emerges here. According to Trudgill, there is a marked difference in the speech of people in working class and middle class occupations. In working class speech, the particular dialect feature he focuses on appears very frequently, but the figures drop very sharply indeed when we look at people in more middle class jobs. In fact, the difference between the figures for upper working class and lower middle class speech is greater, in percentage terms, than for any of the three accent features Trudgill studied. This might suggest that people are even more sensitive to grammatical differences than they are to accent as 'badges' of social class.

## Activity 12

The poem provides several more examples of the features listed in our example – no verb 'to be' in forms like 'I tekking it quiet', and double negatives in 'I ent have no gun' and 'I don't need no axe'. Some words are spelt phonetically and reflect a distinctive pronunciation: 'dem' for 'them' and 'de' for 'the'. You may have noticed some apparent inconsistencies, too: whereas sometimes the past tense is expressed using Standard English grammar ('I didn't graduate'), in the next line a different form ('I immigrate') is used that doesn't include the Standard English ending 'd'. Another way of putting this is to say that the form 'immigrate' is not **marked** for past tense.

Agard clearly identifies Standard English with the power of the English establishment, as represented by Oxford University, its teachers and its dictionary. He also presents it as a language with which he has no wish to identify, and he seems to take delight in using his own low-prestige alternative to attack the language of the powerful.

## Activity 13

All speakers sometimes make mistakes in their language use – slips of the tongue, minor grammatical errors, sentences getting muddled up, and so on – but it would be remarkable if thousands of speakers were simultaneously and consistently making the same mistakes, which is what statement 1 seems to imply. As we have seen, working class speakers are more likely to use non-standard forms, but these are themselves part of the grammatical system of the local dialect rather than 'mistakes'.

Neither is it true to say that non-standard varieties are all derived from a superior, standard version of the language. Many of the dialects we now speak can be traced back to the centuries before the Norman conquest, when Anglo-Saxon and Norse tribes first arrived in Britain from different parts of Germany and Scandinavia. Many distinctive Yorkshire and north-eastern dialect expressions, for example, owe their origins to the presence of the Vikings. So statement 3 offers the most accurate description here.

## Activity 14

You were probably correct in your deduction – it was indeed the east Midlands dialect, spoken in the area including Oxford and Cambridge as well as London, that became the model. After all, this was the dialect used by anyone with power and influence – the court, the church and the printing industry. The dialect we now respectfully see as 'correct' English became so not because it was in any sense a 'purer' or 'better' version of English, but simply because it was the language of power.

## Activity 15

At the start, Mandela uses the pronoun 'us' (a use he sustains ) to unite himself with his audience, creating the sense of unity that is one of the key themes of the speech. It is a tremendously emotional and optimistically forward-looking speech, as it anticipates 'liberty' which he personifies as a newly born infant. He also uses a pair of words that are often found together – 'hope' and 'glory' – and repeats this idea later.

In the third paragraph he lists three aims to try to inspire his listeners – 'ordinary South Africans' – to share the responsibilities for the future: to reinforce humanity's belief in justice, to strengthen its confidence in nobility etc., and to sustain all our hopes for a glorious life. Groups of three are oddly powerful in language, and are often to be found in persuasive texts.

As the speech moves on, his use of language becomes increasingly figurative, referring to South Africa as a body whose wounds are now to be healed, marred by chasms that need to be bridged and the bondage of poverty, deprivation, etc. As usual, the metaphors provide concrete images that express abstract ideas more vividly than the abstractions on their own, and when he talks of leading the country out of the 'valley of darkness', many of his listeners will be aware of the religious register of his language (and a reference to the Psalms of the Old Testament, in particular). The 'road' metaphor is frequently used, and compares the developments of an individual or country to a journey.

The speech builds to a climax with a series of repetitions that become very rhythmical. There are several 'let there be' statements (another biblical echo from the Old Testament, here reminding listeners of another account of the creation of a 'new world' – in the story of Genesis, God says 'Let there be light'). This repetition of phrase or sentence structures is known as **parallelism**. Then there is the repeated 'never' – three times, once again – and the startling contrast between the image of the 'beautiful land' and the 'skunk' to which he compares a South Africa that was for many years shunned by the international community (skunks are shunned because of the vile smell they emit). The climax of the speech works through its simplicity and the shortness of its phrases, as well as the religious reference ('God bless Africa') and the final note of humility with which Mandela thanks his audience.

## Activity 16

The Colman's advertisement uses humour to engage the interest of readers, but still manages to convey its main theme, that the range of Colman's mustards carries an excitingly exotic variety of flavours. Throughout, it puns on the double meaning of 'Far East'. Usually, the phrase refers to the Asian continent but the second part of the initial heading – 'Norwich to be precise' – punctures this expectation with the less exciting sounding East Anglian city. This characteristic humorous trick is repeated when 'the end of the rainbow' is contrasted with 'at the end of the A11'. Note the parallelism between the phrases 'at the end of . . .'.

The advert uses language playfully when it claims that 'Here . . . are flavours that cut the mustard', punning on the colloquial phrase meaning to perform very well, and then when it suggests 'A visit to our Mustard Shop is a must'. Further verbal humour arises in the puns 'the East has its seedy side' and 'That's an Eastern Promise', a phrase some readers might recognise as a cliché used about the Asian continent.

The advertisers link present-day Norwich with an historic past ('The explorers of old'), and the repetition of the words 'exotic' and 'treasures' underlines the central theme of the ad. There is also a strong sense that Colman's is drawing on a wealth of tradition – we are told of the 'long experience in milling, blending and preparing mustard' – note again the grouping of three here.

Many of the sentences are not grammatically complete – 'Norwich to be precise', 'Experience gained over a small matter of 180 years' – which can suggest the impression of a spoken rather than a written text. This last phrase also contains a deliberate irony – we are clearly not meant to think that 180 years is really just a 'small matter', but rather to admire the long tradition associated with the company name, which is repeated several times throughout the text.

## Activity 18

Research suggests that we recognise a number of signs that a speaker is coming to the end of what she or he wants to say:

- *Paralinguistic cues*: the speaker's gestures, posture and eye contact may help us. For example, they may start to lean back in their seat, or sustain prolonged eye contact. Where this happens, it is likely that the person who receives the gaze will be the next speaker.

- *Phonetic and prosodic cues*: the speaker may start to pause, or their intonation may indicate that they are approaching the end of an utterance. Undue hesitancy or non-fluency can therefore act as a turn-taking opportunity.

- *Syntactic cues*: we may recognise the approach of the end of a speaker's sentence.

- *Nomination and direction*: a speaker may explicitly identify the next speaker, as in 'Don't you think, Brian?'

## Activity 19

A's invitation includes some built-in protection in case of rejection. A suggests it is not a thing of huge importance – 'I was just wondering . . .' – so can save face if the answer is 'no'. A also creates a trivial social pretext (having a drink) for the proposed date. The pause before B's reply is awkward. Long pauses are not easily tolerated in English speech – we experience tension and embarrassment when they occur. Here the pause has the effect of suggesting that B is desperately trying to come up with an excuse.

Why not just say 'no', or even 'look, I just don't fancy you'? Because we negotiate many situations involving proposal and acceptance/rejection in such a way as to protect the feelings of those involved. This is one aspect of what is sometimes called the 'politeness principle'.

## Activity 20

The phrase 'First of all' seems to suggest the teacher has a sequenced plan of where the questioning is going, so he or she assumes control of the conversation from the start. Later, phrases like 'let's move on' reinforce this control. The teacher is clearly deciding what gets talked about – Hooke's Law – and for how long, an important indicator of power and conversational dominance.

This dominance is also reflected in the role of the teacher as questioner – none of the pupils asks any questions here; they merely provide the responses. At one point the teacher asks 'Any questions so far?', as if to grant special permission for pupils to intervene at this stage in the conversation. However, none of them does; even if a pupil had intervened, it would probably be to ask a different kind of question to those aked by the teacher. In teacher-talk, the teacher already knows the answers to many of the questions asked; the kinds of question invited from pupils here would be genuine requests for information and clarification. The unusual function of the teacher's questions is not to seek information but to test learning.

For the most part, the pupils' responses are brief – much briefer than the teacher's utterances. Although some powerful people may speak very little, we do tend to grant to people with power and status the right to talk unchallenged for longer. So we need to qualify Grice's maxim of quantity: the length of utterance expected in a conversation is partly determined by the nature of the situation and the power relations of the participants.

The teacher also does some strange things with the responses. Sometimes he or she repeats them or puts them in slightly different words, whereas other responses meet with a judgement ('Right', 'yeah') whose function seems to be to reward or encourage the pupil to continue with the answers. The teacher follows up some responses with 'Why' to push the pupils into thinking the answers through to the logical conclusion the teacher wants them to reach.

## Activity 23

A starts by leading this part of the conversation, and at first B doesn't make a serious attempt to seize the floor or attempt to change the topic. B's first comments – 'Oh', 'mm' and 'Yeah' – are typical **minimal responses**, brief utterances that signal sympathetic encouragement and assure A that B is listening. However, A's speech shows some signs of non-fluency with the two 2-second pauses and the breakdown of grammatical sense ('and (2) being (2) prejudging this bloke'), which prompts B to 'help out' by providing the supportive '//well that's all we can do'. However, by ending this turn with 'did he', a question tag, B in effect yields the floor to A.

A similar pattern can be seen in the next pair of turns. A pauses twice, but B refrains from interrupting, waiting instead until A seems to stumble over a phrase ('deputy's job'), which B helpfully suggests before giving way again. A is allowed to finish, and B adds the supportive agreement 'absolutely'.

So B is certainly behaving in a very co-operative and helpful way, granting the floor and topic control to A, providing supportive minimal responses and even completing A's utterances when A seems to be stumbling.

## Activity 24

At first we notice A's rather cool greeting – 'Ah' – and the forms of address used (A assumes the right to use B's first name, whereas B refers to A as 'Mr Howden'). Some initial pauses may indicate tension; a speaker of equal status might not have waited as long before taking the first turn as B does here. By contrast, A butts in and overlaps with B, and the repeated 'yes' may hint at some impatience. A's control is also reflected by 'take a seat'; the right to dominate a conversation often reflects the right to control the space in which it takes place.

Even though this is a tricky conversation, both participants observe basic politeness strategies, with A pretending that B has come out of choice, as opposed to having been summoned by his boss. After this initial phatic exchange, B takes the initiative ('is there a problem') and A softens his response with the phrase 'I'm afraid', which allows him to imply that although he may have to reprimand B, he regrets having to do so.

However, once the exchange is under way, A asserts his power in many ways. Despite the informality of the form of address ('You'll remember Brian'), the tone is rather formal and severe. B attempts to interrupt as if to clarify what may have happened since their last meeting but A refuses to yield the floor. The attempted interruption having failed, A presses on to the point, though again softening his implied reprimand with the phrase 'I think'. This kind of qualifying phrase is called a **hedge**. B is then reduced to making a minimal response ('Yeah') as A again softens the complaint with 'I'm afraid' before using the euphemistic figure of speech 'not a happy bunny'. B is again cautious about seizing the floor – waiting for 2 seconds before attempting an explanation. Even then, he is allowed only a few moments before A again interrupts with 'in fact . . .' Once again, having been interrupted, B is reduced to accepting his junior status and signals this with a minimal response ('mm').

A continues to soften his language with another hedge ('it does seem'), but it is clear that what is grammatically a declarative ('we need to do some work') is actually an implied rebuke and imperative. There is also the interesting use of the first person plural here; 'we' seems to imply only B, as it his job to put the problem right, but it feels slightly less harsh than the more direct second person 'you'.

So, although A asserts power by controlling the agenda and turn-taking in the conversation, he takes care to soften the harshness of the reprimand and command he is delivering, and the somewhat tense conversation retains a superficial politeness and civility.

## Activity 25

*Same difference?* As a title, 'Master' is relatively rare, being confined to rather formal use when applied to young boys. It has a rather old-fashioned upper class connotation too, as it might have been used by a domestic servant when addressing the young man of a wealthy household. It may have struck you that in its other forms – to master an art, or to achieve mastery, or to be masterful, it implies command and authority. 'Miss', on the other hand, applies not just to young girls but to women who are unmarried. Even mature women may be described as 'Miss', but not always with positive connotations. So although we have a pair of words that appear to be opposites, in fact their usage and connotations are quite different. We call such a difference semantic asymmetry.

The title taken by adult women ('Miss' or 'Mrs') reveals their marital status, something that men do not reveal when entitling themselves 'Mr'. Women are thus defined in terms of their relationship to a man, reflecting their lack of social, economic or personal independence in former times. For this reason, the term 'Ms' was coined as an optional equivalent to the male 'Mr'. However, it is by no means universally used or accepted, and is derided by some as the choice of adult women with feminist inclinations.

*Sticks and stones.* No doubt you already know that English offers a rich source of unpleasant insults to be applied to women – many of which attack them for suggestions of sexual impropriety ('slag', 'slut', 'slapper' etc. – note the interesting phonetic similarities between these terms!). Few such terms are available for abusing promiscuous men, though some, such as 'tart' are beginning to be applied to males in an ironic sort of way. The absence of words to insult promiscuous men is an example of what is called a **lexical gap** – an area of experience or meaning for which the language does not seem to supply a suitable word.

*What's my line?* While 'manager' and 'manageress' appear to describe the same job, in practice there are differences. Would we expect the female boss of a major international company to be called the manageress? Probably not. Actually, the term 'manageress' seems to be reserved for lower status managerial positions, reflecting an expectation that women would not occupy the very highest positions. The ending '-ess' also draws our attention to the gender of the person in an explicit way, which the term 'manager' does not, as is the case with 'author' and 'authoress'. Another way of putting this is to say that the female is the **marked** form. 'Father' and 'mother' seem straightforward enough as nouns, but when we think about their use as verbs ('he fathered three children' and 'she mothered him somewhat'), we discover very different connotations. Fathering is a rather proud act of reproduction which ends with the act of conception. Mothering begins after the birth, and can have connotations of unhealthy protectiveness and smothering.

'Lord' and 'Lady' also reveal an asymmetry in their wider use. 'To lord it' over someone implies authority, status and assertiveness, reflecting the original social and economic power that a 'Lord' enjoyed; however, we cannot say 'to lady it' over someone – 'ladies' don't assert or enforce power; to be 'ladylike' implies a quiet gentility that is in keeping with traditional stereotypes of gracious feminine behaviour. 'Master' we have already touched on; the apparently opposite term 'Mistress' has very different connotations, of course. A married man involved in an extra-marital affair may have a mistress, but a married woman in a similar situation is not said to have 'taken a master'.

## Activity 26

When this test was given to a group of Year 11 school students, the most common choices were 'he' for numbers 1 and 3 and 'she' for 2. Some students spotted the trick, of course, and suggested 'he or she' or 's/he', but the majority assumption was clear. The term 'engineer' is apparently a gender-free term – there is no single word meaning 'female engineer' – but it seems to contain an invisible male marking. 'Nurse' works in the opposite way, so much so that the term 'male nurse' is often used in the same way as people can sometimes be heard referring to a 'lady doctor'; the term 'doctor' is felt to imply maleness. In fact the term 'doctoress' was in use until the nineteenth century.

So, our language often encodes historical assumptions about gender roles and the occupations that men and women follow.

## Activity 27

The 'chairman' issue is still unresolved. Although its use is generic, as with the other examples in the list the word nevertheless encodes an assumption that the person in question – here, the most powerful person on a committee – must be male. Nowadays, if the chairman is a woman, we may feel this to be a contradiction. Nevertheless, 'chairwoman' is not widely used as it uses a marked gender form and thus seems to draw attention to the gender of the person in a way that 'chairman' does not. 'Chairperson' is unwieldy, and as with other cases where 'person' has been substituted for 'man', has been the butt of jokes about 'political correctness'. 'Chair' may be the best alternative as it already exists as a verb ('to chair a meeting'), but its use is by no means universal.

Similar objections apply to many of the other examples. 'Fireman' has now been replaced by the generic 'firefighter' as a job title, 'foreman' is just as likely to be 'supervisor', and 'manning' is just as easily referred to as 'staffing'.

## Activity 29

There seems to be a marked difference between male and female speakers, especially within the lower middle class. Here, more than a quarter of males used the accent feature in question, whereas only a tiny minority of females did so. Of course, what you expected to find would depend on your individual observations and speculation. Many people do report, however, an anecdotal perception that boys and men are more likely to talk with a stronger, more pronounced regional accent than their female counterparts.

There is considerable speculation and disagreement about the reasons for this. One argument is that local accents tend to be associated with working class life, which is also identified with 'tough' masculine qualities. Female speakers are therefore less likely to identify with such values; a male speaker with a strong accent may be described as 'tough', whereas men may describe a woman with a similar accent as 'rough' or unfeminine.

Another theory is that traditional working class social networks based on the workplace serve to 'bond' men more closely than women, and that regional speech becomes one of the ways in which men signal their belonging to this group. Other explanations focus on women's alleged sensitivity to the importance of social mobility and a greater anxiety to make a favourable social impression.

Needless to say, many of these speculations have proved highly controversial.

## Activity 30

The figures from Cheshire's study seem to confirm a similar tendency to Trudgill's study of the Norwich accent among adults. In other words, males are more likely to prefer the non-standard, lower prestige form than females within the same social class.

Interestingly, the researcher tried to relate individuals' use of these dialect forms with their perceived toughness in the eyes of their peers. Sure enough, the boys who used most of the dialectal forms also emerged as those with a high 'toughness' rating. We might conclude that the covert prestige of the dialect seems to be strongest among male speakers because of its association with desirable masculine attributes such as toughness, aggression and even rebelliousness.

## Activity 31

Jennifer Coates writes in her book *Women, Men and Language*:

What effects do such violations of normal turn-taking in conversation have? It seems that after overlaps and especially after interruptions, speakers tend to fall silent. Since most interruptions are produced by men in mixed-sex conversations, the speaker who falls silent is usually a woman. Silence is often a sign of malfunction in conversation. These silences resulted not just from interruptions and overlaps, but also from delayed minimal responses. In mixed-sex conversations male speakers often delayed their minimal responses, signalling a lack of interest in the speaker's topic.

When talking with women, men seem to use interruptions and delayed minimal responses to deny women the right to control the topic of conversation. Men disobey the normal turn-taking rules in order to control topics.

## Activity 33

There is some subject specific language in the reports, though as the writer is directing the texts at an audience which may not share occupationally related jargon, this is limited to readily understood terms such as 'verb constructions' and 'economic concepts'. Rather more interesting is the expression of authority and 'complacent', some of which apply as much to the personality of the student as to his/her work. These may be intensified by 'very' or qualified with a phrase such as 'At a superficial level'. In other places, the writer is using polite understatement, or euphemism – 'to find the course challenging' may be a less hurtful way of suggesting that Jenny is not quite up to her English course, and the hope that she 'should be able to achieve some success' does not sound very confident. The important group of verbs, 'may', 'can', 'must', 'ought' and 'should' (members of the group known as Modal Verbs) indicate the varying degrees of force and certainty in the teachers' pronouncements, but the professional authority of the writers comes through in the formality of the register and the numerous declarative sentences which constitute the reports.

You may have noted the interesting metaphor used by John's Maths teacher – by representing the examiners as opponents who need to be 'defeated' the teacher implies that the examination is at least a game, if not a war!

## Activity 34

Overall, the Otomax advertisement works by mixing two very different registers, those of veterinary science and motoring, and the effect is one of parody, in which the recognisable features of a form are mimicked for comic effect. Nevertheless, the purpose is a serious one – to persuade practising vets to use Otomax in the treatment of a condition known as otitis externa, an inflammation of the outer ear.

The image of the speeding car in the lead slogan, which echoes the claims that car advertisers make for powers of acceleration, stresses the speed with which the product works and its high success rate (93%). The advert sustains the metaphor throughout, describing the drug as a 'marque', and punning on the drug's ability to go 'round even the tightest bend' and to 'stick to the aural canal'. Lexical items such as 'the way it handles' and 'When you open it up' are normally found in the register of motoring, and the advert culminates in borrowing from the same register the notion of 'test driving'.

As well the parody of a car advert, we can recognise several more of the rhetorical features we identified earlier (see page 75). The advert combines factually impressive statistics with vaguer but more emotive claims (it 'really has it all'). It also slips in appropriately impressive technical information ('unique hydrocarbon gel technology', etc.) before using more colloquial and figurative language ('goes round even the tightest bend'), and groups its lists together neatly in threes ('Vets, owners and pets', '3-way combination of clotrimazole, betamethasone and gentamicin'). The text speaks directly to its readers using 'you' throughout.

The ad includes several items from a highly specialised register that is only readily accessible by vets. The condition is otitis externa rather than an ear inflammation, and the reference to the chemical components of the drug uses the appropriate scientific terminology. This language reassures the target audience that the product is being recommended by someone with authority and knowledge in the field, and establishes a professional bond between the advertiser and the potential client.

# MODULE ③ Original Writing

This module counts for 30% of the AS qualification, or 15% of the total A Level marks.

---

**ASSESSMENT OBJECTIVES**

The skills and knowledge that you develop in this module, and that you will be required to demonstrate in your coursework folder, are defined by the examination board's Assessment Objectives. These require that you:

- communicate clearly the knowledge, understanding and insight appropriate to the study of language, using appropriate terminology and accurate and coherent written expression
  (5% of the final AS mark; $2\frac{1}{2}$% of the final A Level mark)

- demonstrate expertise and accuracy in writing for a variety of specific purposes and audiences, drawing on knowledge of linguistic features to explain and comment on choices made
  (20% of the final AS mark; 10% of the final A Level mark)

- understand, discuss and explore concepts and issues relating to language in use
  (5% of the final AS mark; $2\frac{1}{2}$% of the final A Level mark)

---

## Coursework

In this module, you must produce a coursework folder. This should contain two pieces of work plus a commentary. Your two pieces of coursework may be in any form or genre. Each piece must be clearly differentiated in terms of primary purpose, audience and form. The total length of the two pieces together should be between 1500 and 3000 words.

The commentary on your work should be approximately 1000 words in total. In it, you need to analyse and review:

- your choice of vocabulary and syntactic structures

- your style of writing

- the overall structure and organisation of your text

- any changes made during drafting and redrafting

The marks for this module will be added together and scaled to reflect the weighting of 60:40 between the two pieces and the commentary.

This is the part of your English Language AS or A Level where you can make use of and develop your own skills as a writer. In your coursework folder you need to provide evidence of your ability to write for different audiences and for different purposes. You must also show in your commentary that you were aware, when writing, of the need to adapt your language to the requirements of your audience and the purpose of your text.

The best way to discover how writers produce effective (or not so effective) texts is to examine examples. This module focuses upon the examination of texts taken from a variety of sources, including other students' coursework folders. You will examine the following types of text:

- writing to entertain

- writing to persuade

- writing to inform

- writing advice and/or instructions

- commentary writing

In the sections devoted to each of these categories you will find texts written for different audiences and for different purposes. In each case, you will examine the individual techniques of the writers and any common characteristics of writing for a particular purpose or audience. Your examination of the ways in which writers use language to achieve a variety of effects will help you when producing your own original writing coursework and when writing your commentaries. Each section includes suggestions for written tasks, so you can try for yourself some of the techniques you have learnt.

*It is important that you keep all your written notes for future reference.* You must include all rough drafts, and the notes that you make on the style and techniques of other writers, in your coursework folder.

## Developing your writing skills

In this section we look at some of the basic techniques a writer uses to create specific effects. In particular, we'll be looking at how to build up awareness of character and how to make clear an attitude to a text. For this reason, most of the texts in this section are fiction texts, and many of them are written in the first person – writing from one's own experience is a good way to 'get into the swing of things'.

### Who is your reader?

Before we look at creating characters and investigate the tone of pieces of writing, we need to look closely at the people involved in a piece of writing. Writing is a piece of communication between a writer and a reader. Different readers bring different assumptions, attitudes and expectations to the texts they read; and it is by understanding and exploiting these that writers become successful and effective. Your awareness of who is going to read the texts you write forms the basis of your assessment in this module.

Whenever we write we make certain assumptions about our readers, particularly if they belong to our age group, have the same type of cultural background as ourselves or do the same type of work as us. We might assume, for instance, that they have seen the same films and read the same books – or at least have heard of them. We might assume that they have similar tastes in humour or in what they find ridiculous. This type of shared reference can provide us with a useful form of shorthand – we don't have to spell out exactly what we are driving at.

The following extract appeared in *Loaded* in September 1999. *Loaded* is a magazine aimed at 'youngish' men and the language is often informal, using colloquial and, sometimes, taboo words and expressions. The extract is part of an article detailing the experiences of five men on a cycling holiday in Ireland. At several points the writer assumes that his readers will be familiar with certain references to film, TV, advertising and children's reading. He also makes use of stereotypical imagery in his descriptions of one of the people he met while on holiday.

## Blazing Sandals – Five go on a cycling holiday in Ireland by mistake

AFTER AN attempt to view the famous cliffs of Moher, sadly souped in fog, we arrive in Doolin. God tilts a hill downwards, opening the mind's shed doors to the freewheel adrenaline of landscape rush. A bumpy, butt-hammering 30-mile-an-hour trip. Luke, or 'swiney' because he eats chocolate and pies, bursts a tyre. We leave him and continue, eventually ditching the bikes by a stream to sulk in a pub.

We phone Ronan to tell him we've had enough and insist he gives us a lift to the next B&B. Day one ends without pride or adventure. Like the shopkeeper in *Mr Benn*, Ronan appears and changes our surroundings. He delivers us to a house built on a prehistoric slab of limestone now called Lisdoonvarna. It is here we meet Joe.

Joe dresses like us and owns a bog full of peat. Through his greying, half-grown Captain Birdseye beard he speaks Irish at the speed of a tin whistle. Joy and wisdom, and regular requests for a 'pint-a-Arrrp', flow from his lips. He takes us to a pub where Man Utd's dramatic treble gives currency to a new saying: 'sick as a German'.

## ACTIVITY 1

C3.1A, C3.2, WO3.2, LP3.2

In pairs, find examples, in the title and the extract, of language that assumes a shared cultural background. Look for examples of references to films, books and TV programmes; pastimes or interests that readers probably share; and images that readers may expect to find.

Which words or groups of words are used to create the following effects: (1) damp, wet weather; (2) a sudden, downward movement; (3) speed; and (4) an uncomfortable ride? And which expressions are used to depict the 'Irishness' of Joe? Why do you think the writer refers to these things in these ways?

Now read the commentary on page 143.

Elsewhere in the article the writer mentions 'Father Ted', 'Oxfam', 'Sue Ryder shops', 'Ronnie Corbett', 'Bobby Ewing hair', *The Magic Roundabout*, *The Wizard of Oz*, *The Goodies* and 'Queen'. Do these references mean anything to you?

## ACTIVITY 2                                                    C3.1A

In pairs or small groups, discuss those areas of modern culture that you assume an audience of your peers would find familiar but an older audience would not.

In what type of writing could you make use of such references? How would you use them? Would it be to create humour or irony, or as a shorthand way of describing something or someone?

## Creating characters

As well as creating a relationship between the writer and the reader based on a shared understanding, the writer also creates a relationship between his characters and the reader. This is most obviously the case when the text is written in the first person and the speaker directly addresses the reader.

A character is often established by the deliberate 'misuse' of a shared culture between the speaker and his reader. As you will see when you read the extract from *The Secret Diary of Adrian Mole Aged 13¾*, Sue Townsend makes Adrian display his values, and it is the difference between his assumptions and the reader's that creates much of the humour.

However, it is not simply their culture that reveals the nature of a character in a text; it is also the language that they use. In this section, we look at two writers who both use the first person and who use genres that are related in that they are often personal and intimate (the diary and the letter). Despite these similarities, each writer creates a very different impression of their character. This is because the specific language patterns of the character as well as the culture and assumptions they reveal help to build a clear picture of the character in the reader's mind.

As you read each extract try to think about what is similar and what is different about the use of language in each.

### THE SECRET DIARY OF ADRIAN MOLE AGED 13³/₄

Thursday March 12th

Woke up this morning to find my face covered in huge red spots. My mother said they were caused by nerves but I am still convinced that my diet is inadequate. We have been eating a lot of boil-in-the-bag stuff lately. Perhaps I am allergic to plastic. My mother rang Dr Gray's receptionist to make an appointment, but the earliest he can see me is next Monday! For all he knows I could have lassa fever and be spreading it all around the district! I told my mother to say that I was an emergency case but she said I was 'over-reacting as usual'. She said a few spots didn't mean I was dying. I couldn't believe it when she said she was going to work as usual. Surely her child should come before her job?

I rang my grandma and she came round in a taxi and took me to her house and put me to bed. I am there now. It is very clean and peaceful. I am wearing my dead grandad's pyjamas. I have just had a bowl of barley and beef soup. It is my first proper nourishment for weeks.

I expect there will be a row when my mother comes home and finds that I have gone. But frankly, my dear diary, I don't give a damn.

## ACTIVITY 3

Who is the intended audience for the extract above? What is it about the subject matter and the language that leads you to form your conclusions?

What can you tell about the supposed writer of the diary from the language he uses in this entry? What sort of mood is he in, and how does he feel about his mother's attitude?

Look at the use of exclamation marks and rhetorical questions. What purpose do these serve?

Now read the commentary on page 144.

The following text comes from *The Color Purple* by Alice Walker and deals with something altogether more disturbing.

### *You better not never tell nobody but God. It'd kill your mammy.*

Dear God,

I am fourteen years old. ~~I am~~ I have always been a good girl. Maybe you can give me a sign letting me know what is happening to me.

Last spring after little Lucious come I heard them fussing. He was pulling on her arm. She say It too soon, Fonso, I ain't well. Finally he leave her alone. A week go by, he pulling on her arm again. She say Naw, I ain't gonna. Can't you see I'm already half dead, an all of these chilren.

She went to visit her sister doctor over Macon. Left me to see after the others. He never had a kine word to say to me. Just say You gonna do what your mammy wouldn't. . . .

## ACTIVITY 4                                                C3.1A

In pairs, use the following questions to help you examine the lexis, graphology and grammar of the preceding extract in order to understand how Alice Walker has created an impression of the speaker's character. Individually, make detailed notes about the ideas discussed. Afterwards, read the commentary on page 145.

See Module 1 to review graphology (page 18) and phonology (page 27).

*Lexis and grammar*: how does the language use differ from standard written English? Why has this style of language been used?

*Graphology*: what is distinctive about the appearance on the page of this extract?

*Character*: what do we learn from the lexis, grammar and graphology of this extract about the writer of the letter? Why is she writing to God?

This module's emphasis is on identifying techniques, so that you can use them in your own writing. You have seen how the choice of a character's lexis and grammar can build up a picture of that character. You have also seen how the use of the first person creates an intimate, personal relationship between character and reader.

## ACTIVITY 5                        C3.1A, C3.3, LP3.2, LP3.3

You are going to create a character who will 'write' a fictional story in letter or diary form.

First, make notes on the background, personal characteristics and situation of the character you wish to create, then describe their language style. Think about what lexis they will use, whether they will write in Standard English and their personal language habits. How will you use punctuation and grammar to reveal their character, and how will you demonstrate their level of education? Write down how these will help to build a picture for the reader.

Then, in pairs or small groups, share your ideas and whether you think these will work. Keep a note of positive and negative comments and criticisms as well as any changes of plan. Remember to keep all your notes and preparatory plans – if you later decide to develop any class work for your coursework folder you will need them for the actual writing and for your commentaries.

Write your diary entries or your letter in no more than 250 words. If you choose the letter form you may need to think about the recipient of the letters too; will that person's replies be part of the story?

So far, your work in this module will have helped you to think about the writer's craft. How does a writer achieve a relationship with their audience and use language to develop character? The pieces of writing you have done have been relatively short, but could be developed into longer pieces suitable for your coursework folder.

Now we are going to look in turn at the five different reasons for writing introduced at the beginning of this module, and how these purposes affect a writer's choices of approach.

# Writing to entertain

One of the pieces you could produce for your coursework folder is one whose principal purpose is to entertain. It could take one of a number of forms: a short story, a radio script, a stand-up comedy routine . . . For the purposes of this section, however, we are going to look at short stories and, in particular, at the features of different types of story.

## Genre

When we use the word 'genre' we are really only saying that a text is of a certain *kind*.

So we have the genres of prose, of fiction, of poetry and of drama. Each genre has its own conventions or rules – in relation to graphology or layout, for instance. Other characteristics are obviously important, but there can be overlap: one genre can and sometimes does use devices more usually associated with another.

If we take poetry as an example, we might describe some of the characteristic devices of the poet as the use of figurative language, rhyme, metre and sound effects such as alliteration and onomatopoeia. These are only some of the more obvious language choices available to a poet, but even here you can see that some of these are also used by writers of other genres. Novelists use figurative language such as metaphor; we all use it in everyday speech. Advertisers use alliteration and rhyming effects. Poets can tell stories in narrative verse and dramatists can use rhyme, metre and any of the other devices – look at Shakespeare.

Within each of these genres there is a whole range of sub-genres, each of which carries grammatical patterns and lexical choices that signal to the audience what type of text they are reading or watching. By signalling the sub-genre within which he or she is writing, a writer sets up various expectations among the audience that are then fulfilled or exploited to achieve a particular effect.

In this section, we look at three different sub-genres of prose fiction and identify the characteristics of each one, then go on to look at how writers can play with these.

# The structure of fairy tales

The table shows the plot development of the well-known fairy tale 'Snow White and the Seven Dwarfs'.

| Structure of plot | 'Snow White' |
|---|---|
| Good and bad characters established | Snow White lives with her wicked stepmother |
| Problem | Stepmother wants Snow White killed |
| Development of problem | Stepmother finds Snow White living with the dwarfs and gives her a poisoned apple |
| Solution of problem | A prince saves Snow White |
| Resolution | The prince and Snow White get married |

If you look at enough fairy tales, you may well find that many have similarities in their basic outlines. This type of story adopts a formulaic approach.

## ACTIVITY 6

C3.1A, C3.2, LP3.2

Think of another fairy tale that you know. Does the plot follow the same structure as that outlined above? Are there any other similarities, such as the type of characters, how many characters appear, when they are introduced and what status they have?

Discuss the similarities and differences between the fairy tale you have thought of and the ones other members of your group have chosen.

The formulaic approach is not restricted to fairy stories; it can be found in genre fiction of all types. The existence of a formula or recipe need not mean that there is no originality, but it can lead to predictable storylines and characterisation. As soon as a reader recognises that they are reading a certain type of story, they will expect the plot to develop in particular ways and to be introduced to various characters.

## ACTIVITY 7

C3.3

Make a list of the main features of a fairy story, using the table for the Snow White plot structure together with any notes you made for Activity 6. Use your list to plan a fairy story of your own. You do not need to write the story as long as you have shown how the plot will develop and what characters will be introduced when.

Once again, *remember to keep all your notes and your plot outline* if you are going to develop this work into a piece of coursework.

The existence of certain characteristics within sub-genres can be very useful to writers, not only in meeting the expectations they set up but also exploiting those expectations. Once you understand the expected features you can surprise your reader by not meeting them, or by exaggerating them in order to create a specific effect. We'll look at how some writers have been able to parody or send up a sub-genre later on. First, though, we'll identify the features of some other prose fiction sub-genres.

## Romantic fiction

There is a sub-genre of romantic fiction, easily recognised in the books published by Mills & Boon, which often makes use of stereotypical descriptions of physical attractiveness and draws upon clichéd expressions for emotions felt by the characters. The storylines always follow a similar pattern. For instance, a young woman, alone in the world and usually quite innocent and sexually inexperienced, moves from a small town to the big city to earn a living. She meets a young man to whom she is physically and emotionally attracted, and another for whom she feels nothing but loathing because he is arrogant/distant/cruel or any number of other reasons. He is nearly always of a high social status – such as a doctor, a surgeon, a top businessman – and is 'masculine' in appearance. There is usually another woman involved who is a 'rival' in some way. After many trials and tribulations, the first young woman realises that she loves the man she thought she hated, but now she thinks he hates her. Needless to say, they are eventually united in love and all is well. Those who have been unkind to our 'heroine' are 'punished' in some way and everything ends well for her – she has a man!

Sometimes these novels are set in exotic locations, sometimes in hospitals, and occasionally the heroine is a middle-aged divorcée or widow attempting to begin life anew.

The following text is an extract from chapter 3 of a Silhouette Desire novel entitled *Winter Heat*. The female character has previously admired her new next door neighbour from afar and has now decided to introduce herself.

Drawing closer, she could see his profile; it was carefully defined. His pronounced jawline suggested stubbornness, but the nose was well shaped and blended into the craggy contours of his cheeks and the hard angle of his jaw. She was conscious of the strength he exuded, yet she experienced a tingle of fear along her back. Her study concluded with one word: dangerous, an exceedingly dangerous man to avoid at all cost.

Again he was wearing jeans, old and worn ones that hadn't held a crease in months, if ever, but that fit him like a glove. Fearing she would be caught staring where she shouldn't, Alison kept her eyes pinned above the waist. Even at that, she got more than she bargained for. His flannel work shirt, equally as worn, was open down the front, allowing her to see an abundance of wiry chest hair. She took a sudden breath.

Without warning, he raised his head and their eyes met. For an instant Alison had trouble breathing. She didn't realise until later that it was the glacier coldness of his eyes that robbed her of her breath.

He straightened to full height and leaned on the posthole digger. He was tall, taller than he'd first appeared, towering over her five foot six by at least eight inches. She found herself further captivated by the way he moved, like a well-honed athlete, effortless and graceful. He also had the body of one: halfback shoulders tapered to a flat stomach, trim hips and powerful thighs.

But the unrelenting coldness of his eyes continued to chill her to the marrow, though she didn't flinch under his stare. Suddenly feeling the need to say something, anything that would break the tension, she murmured inanely,

'Hi.'

He leaned more heavily on the tool and angled his head, wariness now replacing the coldness.

'Hello.'

Alison responded to the rich, deep timbre of his voice as quickly as she'd responded to him. She felt warm all over.

## ACTIVITY 8                                                    C3.2

After reading the extract carefully, decide what view is presented of the male character and how this is achieved. Look carefully at the description of his physical attributes, his actions and the female character's response to him. What do we learn about the female character? Note the language used to describe her emotions and responses. What does this suggest?

Examine the connotations of the novel title (*Winter Heat*) and the name of the collection to which it belongs (Silhouette Desire). Now read the commentary on page 146.

## ACTIVITY 9                              C3.1, C3.3, LP3.2, LP3.3

Collect examples of this type of fiction (Silhouette, Mills & Boon etc.). They are easily available from libraries and second-hand book shops. Make notes on the similarities, including storylines and characterisation. Use your notes to plan an outline of a romantic novel of this type.

Now write one chapter from the novel you have planned. It doesn't have to be the first chapter. In writing your chapter, attempt to replicate the type of descriptions and general language you found in your survey. In groups, discuss whether you found it difficult to sustain the style. Compare your chapter with those written by others in your group.

Remember that you will need to keep any notes for this activity in case you decide to develop this for your coursework folder.

## Exploiting expectations

We have seen that different sub-genres of fiction have different characteristics. The reader knows what to expect, and part of the pleasure in reading is to have these expectations met. However, rigid adherence to the characteristics of a certain sub-genre can also make a piece of writing predictable and clichéd. To make their writing more interesting, innovative and challenging, many writers play with the characteristics of a genre, creating an element of surprise by not entirely satisfying the expectations that their readers bring to the text.

### Same story?

Below are two versions of the 'Snow White' story. You may well be familiar with both. The first is the traditional form and the second is in the form of a humorous verse, written for the modern child. Read the two versions and complete the activity which follows.

### 'Snowdrop', by Jacob and Wilhelm Grimm

It was the middle of winter, and the snowflakes were falling from the sky like feathers. Now a Queen sat sewing at a window framed in black ebony, and as she sewed she looked out upon the snow.

Suddenly she pricked her finger and three drops of blood fell on to the snow. And the red looked so lovely on the white that she thought to herself: if only I had a child as white as snow and as red as blood, and as black as the wood in the window frame! Soon after she had a daughter, whose hair was as black as ebony, while her cheeks were as red as blood, and her skin as white as snow, so she was called Snowdrop. But when the child was born, the Queen died. A year after, the king took another wife. She was a handsome woman, but proud and overbearing, and she could not endure that anyone should surpass her in beauty. She had a miraculous looking-glass, and when she stood before it and looked at herself, she used to say:

'Mirror, Mirror on the wall,
Who is the fairest of us all?'

Then the Glass answered:

'Queen, thou'rt fairest of them all.'

Then she was contented, for she knew that the looking-glass spoke the truth.

But Snowdrop grew up and became more and more beautiful, so that when she was seven years old, she was as beautiful as the day, and far surpassed the Queen. Once, when she asked her Glass:

'Mirror, Mirror on the wall,
Who is the fairest of us all?'

It answered:

'Queen, thee fairest here I hold,
But Snowdrop fairer a thousandfold.'

Then the Queen was horror-struck, and turned green and yellow with jealousy.

## 'Snow-White and the Seven Dwarfs'

When little Snow-White's mother died,
The king, her father, up and cried,
'Oh, what a nuisance! What a life!
'Now I must find another wife!'
(It's never easy for a king
To find himself that sort of thing.)
He wrote to every magazine
And said, 'I'm looking for a Queen.'
At least ten thousand girls replied
And begged to be the royal bride.
The king said with a shifty smile,
'I'd like to give each one a trial.'
However, in the end he chose
A lady called Miss Maclahose,
Who brought along a curious toy
That seemed to give her endless joy –
This was a mirror framed in brass,
A MAGIC TALKING LOOKING-GLASS.
Ask it something day or night,
It always got the answer right.
For instance, if you were to say,
'Oh Mirror, what's for lunch today?'
The thing would answer in a trice,
'Today it's scrambled eggs and rice.'
Now every day, week in week out,
The spoiled and stupid Queen would shout,
'Oh Miror Mirror on the wall,
'Who is the fairest of them all?'
The Mirror answered every time,
'Oh Madam, you're the Queen sublime.
'You are the only one to charm us,
'Queen, you are the cat's pyjamas.'
For ten whole years the silly Queen
Repeated the absurb routine.
Then suddenly, one awful day,
She heard the Magic Mirror say,

'From now on, Queen, you're *Number Two*.
'*Snow-White* is prettier than you!'
The Queen went absolutely wild.
She yelled, 'I'm going to scrag that child!
'I'll cook her flaming goose! I'll skin 'er!
'I'll have her rotten guts for dinner!'

## ACTIVITY 10

What aspects of language use has Roald Dahl focused upon when adapting this story? How have the changes affected the tone of the story? Is the audience for the story the same as in the original?

Now read the commentary on page 146.

## ACTIVITY 11                    WO3.1, WO3.1

Ask yourself how this story might continue. In pairs, continue the 'revolting rhyme', taking care to maintain the rhythm and tone of this extract. Before you start, you may want to write a plan of the traditional story as a guide.

Are there any other traditional stories or myths which you could adapt in this way? Avoid those already adapted by Roald Dahl.

Traditional stories and story-lines can be and have been adapted in many ways. For instance, one writer at least (James Finn Garner) has published a politically correct version of this story and others in a collection called *Politically Correct Bedtime Stories.* Notions of political correctness have made a huge impact on language use in recent years. Vocabulary related to such things as colour, race, gender, age, occupation and much more has undergone subtle (and not so subtle) modification as we have become, or been made, more aware of the inbuilt bias of some words and phrases.

In the politically correct version of this story, for example, Garner focuses upon such things as physical descriptions and semantics, especially the connotations of certain colours and nominations (such as 'stepmother'). He also makes use of understatement: Snow-White is described as 'not at all unpleasant to look at', in contrast to the hyperbole of the original 'as beautiful as the day'.

 Look back at the section on language and gender in Module 2 (page 84)

## ACTIVITY 12

In pairs, discuss how the following words or phrases could be seen as having inbuilt bias: wiatress; old age pensioner; disabled; chairman.

What alternative terms could you use in order not to give offence?

Now read the commentary on page 47

In pairs, discuss how the traditional story of 'Snow White' might be adapted to create a politically correct version.

## Writing within a sub-genre

Writers who play with readers' expectations in a certain genre do not simply rewrite existing stories, of course. It is *new* pieces of writing that play with expectations that often provide the most effective examples of this approach.

You are going to write a short story of about 500 words. It must demonstrate that you are aware of the conventions of the sub-genre within which you are writing, but play with those conventions to achieve a surprising effect. You could write a piece of romantic fiction in which the girl and boy do not get together, a ghost story written from the point of view of the ghost rather than of the person being haunted, a horror story, a science fiction story, and so on. Whichever you choose, it is important to set up the story using that sub-genre's conventions so that your reader knows what to expect; then you can alter the nature of the piece.

| **ACTIVITY 13** | **C3.2, C3.3** |
|---|---|

Choose the type of story you're going to write. It can be one of those already mentioned or another of your own choosing. Think of stories that you have read within that sub-genre, and make a note of what they have in common. Think about: the structure of the plot, the different types of characters in the story, the amount of dialogue compared to the amount of description, what person (first, third, etc.) these stories are normally written in, and any common narrative devices (time shifts, flashbacks . . .).

When you have listed the conventions of your chosen sub-genre, plan your own story. Focus on the characters, the development of the plot and the language you will use. Now think about how you can alter the conventions you have identified. Which will you use, and which will you exploit? Make a note of your thoughts.

Write out your story and show it to a partner. Ask for feedback about how effective it is, and make a note of their comments, both positive and negative. Rewrite the story to take account of any criticisms you received. Remember to keep all your drafts and notes for your coursework folder.

# Writing to persuade

Throughout this module and the AS Language course, you will see how language use varies according to the writer's purposes and audience. So far in this module we have looked mostly at fictional writing; for the most part this is written to entertain. However, there are many types of writing that have other primary purposes: to persuade, to inform, to instruct . . . . Each of these purposes for writing can be characterised by certain language features. In this section we look at persuasive writing.

# Features of persuasive writing

The techniques used to persuade depend to some extent on what it is the writer is trying to persuade us to do. Does the writer want us to buy something or to do something – or to think something and adopt a certain point of view?

## ACTIVITY 14      C3.1A, WO3.2, WO3.3

In a group, brainstorm various forms of writing that have persuasion as their main purpose. Write your suggestions in the table opposite. The first one has been started for you.

When you have a list of forms of writing, discuss what language features are commonly used in each type in order to persuade the reader. Think about grammar, graphology and lexis. Make a note of each one in the second column of the table, as in the example.

| Form of writing | Features of language |
| --- | --- |
| advert | use of imperative ('Buy now!')<br>lots of positive adjectives<br>large heading to attract attention<br>use of questions<br>. . . |
| | |
| | |

Some of the techniques we could expect to find in writing that aims to persuade are:

- emotive language – language used in a way that appeals to the emotions
- question and answer techniques – the writer sets a question or a problem and then offers an answer or solution
- rhetorical questions
- hyperbole (exaggeration)
- reference to 'expert' studies – facts and figures
- figurative language – metaphor and simile
- contrasts – we do this, but they don't (or they do that)
- indications of stress upon a word – italics, block capitals, underlining etc.
- asides and emphases indicated through punctuation – brackets, exclamation marks, question marks . . .
- repetition of words and phrases, or of grammatical structures

This list is not prescriptive nor is it complete, and you will probably be able to add to it from the work you did in Activity 14. Also look back at the section 'The power of language' in Module 2 (pages 73–6). Some of the techniques are used in the following extract, which aims to persuade its readers to take a certain attitude. As you read it, try to identify the techniques used.

# KOREANS MAKE A WORLD CUP DOG'S DINNER

(THE *GUARDIAN*, 30 SEPTEMBER 1999)

Among British animal lovers, dogs enjoy a high profile, and rightly so. The esteem in which our four-legged friends are held has its roots in pre-Roman times. When Phoenician traders first reported on the remote islands they knew as Thule, of all our impressive array of exports (woad, trinkets, mead, second-hand chariot wheels) our hunting dogs were most highly prized. Mad dogs and Englishmen have become inextricably linked. In our world view, a dog is a man's best friend – an idea of ours that the Americans (as in so much else) have heartily embraced. After all, what did Bill Clinton do at the height of his domestic difficulties?

He went out and bought a frisky, black variety called Buddy, now employed as White House First Dog and walking comfort zone.

The South Koreans love dogs too, but in a different way. They like eating them. Dog-meat, by ancient belief, is held to delay ageing and enhance sexual prowess. In Korea, the term 'puppy fat' conceals saucy delights. So the decision by the agriculture ministry in Seoul to extend a ban on human dog-food until after the 2002 World Cup finals appears impressively altruistic. The authorities reportedly fear a national embarrassment should visiting fans take exception to canine cuisine. Menus featuring Alsatian à la mode

or springer spaniel stew might offend. This is sensitive stuff.

But is it necessary? After all, the Norwegians will persist in eating whales. Do we ostracise them? Not really. The Italians sup on song-birds, which is quite reprehensible, but they suffer no reprisals (though, hopefully, indigestion). The French egregiously eat horses, but this may be because their thoroughbreds have little other use. Do we boycott the Dordogne? We do not. The truth is, the deplorable eating habits of foreigners are beyond our control. Perhaps we should boycott the World Cup? Sadly, given the way our national teams have gone to the dogs, this may not be an option.

## ACTIVITY 15   C3.2

Work out the main message of the article, and decide who it is written for. How is language used to persuade the audience of the writer's view? Decide how many of the techniques itemised earlier are employed by the writer, and how effective they are in this context.

Now read the commentary on pages 147–148.

## ACTIVITY 16   C3.3

Write a piece of journalism of about 300 words to persuade your reader that Korea should extend the ban on selling dog meat for the duration of the World Cup. Assume a similar readership as for the *Guardian* piece you have just read.

Before you begin writing, make a note of the type of language that is appropriate for this audience and the techniques you will use to persuade them of your point of view. Show your finished article to a partner and get their feedback. Rewrite the article to take on board their comments, and keep all your notes and drafts for your coursework folder.

## Writing for a sympathetic audience

It is always easier to persuade an audience of a point of view if they are already sympathetic to the perspective on life that gave rise to it. Once the basic premise on which an audience forms its view is established, a writer can build on this and gain the audience's agreement on a particular subject.

Here is an article that was printed in the *Countryman's Weekly*, attacking the RSPCA's campaign against hunting. Because of where it was printed, the writer could be pretty sure that he would get a sympathetic hearing, so can move his readers with him to accept his point of view.

# RSPCA KILLER PACK

YOU NEVER THOUGHT you'd see the day this headline appeared? Well, it is with great trepidation that I announce that the RSPCA is taking up hunting.

No, this is not old Gunner being offensive to this animal 'welfare' group, but I do like to provoke a little thought.

In fact, the RSPCA's pack will consist of 800 hounds. They will be released from kennels to kill wantonly and indiscriminately and cause the most diabolical suffering.

There will be no closed season, babies in the nest will be killed slowly and painfully, and there will be no Huntsman or hunt firearm to ensure a quick end should the need arise.

## Huge Pack

In fact, the RSPCA will not even accompany this huge pack or accept any responsibility for the hounds after it has released them. There will be no code of conduct, no hunt debate or political argument and the animal rights industry will not raise a murmur.

Think old Gunner has lost his marbles, do you? That may be

true, but everything I have said is correct, except that you will now need to substitute the hounds I have mentioned for cats.

Cats, you see, are not politically incorrect and the subject of huge cash donations to political parties. And the RSPCA have removed 800 cats from Hillgrove Farm, a cat breeding establishment said to sell them for experimentation. They will be neutered, taken to RSPCA centres and the society will be appealing for homes for them. They will then kill wantonly.

Carla Lane, a well-meaning television script writer, said it was a wonderful day for animals.

Without wishing to throw a spanner in the works, could I point out that cats kill almost 80 per cent of all wild animals, there is a catch-to-kill interval of 30 minutes and they regularly kill endangered and protected species. Their food supply is supplemented so that they remain in good condition for the hunt.

A leading researcher in this field concludes: 'Legislation and research focused on this (killer cats) would provide the largest single reduction in wild animal

suffering. Simply reducing predation by cats during the sensitive breeding months of April to July could reduce wildlife deaths by 100 million a year, the equivalent in one year to banning all hunting with dogs for 200 years.'

On a scale of suffering the wanton killing by the domestic cat comes second only to the deliberate spreading of myxomatosis among rabbits. Ironically the latter was introduced as an alternative to traditional forms of pest control after the Second World War.

I'm not saying the cat farm was a good thing or a bad thing nor condemning the RSPCA's involvement, because with animal rights terrorists involved the whole thing could have got out of hand at Hillgrove. But an organisation cannot condone the keeping of cats and oppose fox hunting without being deeply hypocritical and in breach of its own stated aims. There is, consequently, some dispute as to how fraudulent this might make the society's requests for public donations.

Gunner will now make a run for it before some miffed RSPCA inspector sees me and sets his dogs loose.

## ACTIVITY 17

**C3.1A, C3.2**

Discuss how the writer establishes common ground with the reader. Think about how he establishes familiarity between himself as the speaker of the article and the reader, and how he sets up the contrast between 'us' and the 'them' of the RSPCA. Notice too how his language matches the way that his readers probably use language.

The writer uses humour to get across his message. How is the humour created, and what effect does it have – and how does the language ensure that his message is not lost in the humour? Also think about the effect of the use of statistics, and the repetition of the term 'In fact'.

What is the effect of the last sentence? Now read the commentary on page 148.

## ACTIVITY 18

**C3.3, C3.1A, LP3.2**

Choose a topical subject in an area of debate and disagreement. Write an article for a newspaper or journal whose readership will be generally sympathetic to your viewpoint, if not necessarily 100 per cent in agreement with everything that you say. You have to persuade your audience to accept your point of view.

It is up to you to pick a type of publication suitable for your subject. Here are some suggestions: the underpayment of nurses (in a medical or health magazine); the lack of childcare facilities (in a magazine aimed at working women); the need for higher and more widespread student discounts (in a magazine aimed at students).

Before you start writing, think about:

- how you will establish a relationship with your reader to put you both on the same side of the argument

- what techniques you will use to persuade them of your point of view

- the tone of your piece and, if you use humour, how you will get the serious points across

- the best balance between facts and figures, anecdote and argument

You may need to research your chosen topic in order to establish facts that you can use in your piece of writing. When your piece is at the first draft stage, read each other's work (in small groups) and provide feedback on how successful your persuasive devices have been.

## Awareness of audience

As in all writing, the author of a piece of persuasive writing will vary the language and techniques depending on the audience.

Here is a pair of film reviews. The first one is taken from *Marie Claire* and is written for an adult audience; the second is from *Live and Kicking* and is aimed at a younger audience.

---

# STAR WARS: EPISODE 1 – THE PHANTOM MENACE

In a galaxy far, far away . . . there was a giant multiplex called Planet Lucas. Life forms from all over the universe visited, carrying trillions of ecus (extra-terrestrial currency units) to pay homage to the great cash cow of the Force, *Star Wars*. The message of the Force was clear: buy your Ewan McGregor bendy doll, buy your light saber and pop-up books. Buy the myth. Buy the hype. George Lucas's prequel to his space saga takes place a generation prior to the original and focuses on Jedi knights Qui-Gon Jinn (Liam Neeson) and his pupil Obi Wan-Kenobi (McGregor), as they try to save a peaceful planet from its trading enemies. We're also introduced to the young Anakin Skywalker – before he fathers Luke, joins the dark side and becomes Darth Vader. Befitting Lucas's interests (and limitations) as a director, the computer-generated effects are wondrous, but the human characters are given less animation than their cuddly creature counterparts.

---

# WILD, WILD WEST

Will Smith, Salma Hayek, Kenneth Branagh, Kevin Klein

Funky Will Smith puts on his cowboy boots for his latest serving of adventure. James West (Smith) teams up with fellow cowboy special agent Artemus Gordon (Klein) to do battle with the v. evil Dr Loveless (Branagh) with the clumsy help of Rita (Hayek). Using all their weird and whacky inventions, loadsa luck and Will's sexy bum, they track down bad guys and give 'em lots of grief. Power-mad Dr Loveless is intent on taking over the US of A, and it's up to our big Willie to save the day again! Everyone ends up loving Mr Smith, but will he keep his good looks? The acting's cheesy and the plot's paper-thin, but Loveless's evil world-crushing invention is total crackerjack.

## ACTIVITY 19

For each of the reviews, identify the language features that make them appropriate for their audience, and describe the effect these features have. What techniques does the writer use to persuade the reader of his opinion?

What would you change in the first review to make it suitable for a teenage readership? What would you change in the second review to make it suitable for an adult readership? Now read the commentary on page 149.

## ACTIVITY 20

**C3.3, LP3.2, LP3.3**

Write two reviews for the same film for different target audiences. Aim the first at a teenage audience and the second at a well-educated adult audience. In each case, determine how you will establish a relationship with the target audience, and decide which persuasive devices would be most effective. What language features will you use in each, and how will they differ? How much opinion and how much fact will you include?

Write your reviews and get feedback from other members of your group.

## Writing to inform

Another purpose for writing is to pass on information, and, just as writing to persuade uses various features and techniques related to its purpose, so does writing to inform. Informative writing is all around us: in news reports, encyclopaedia entries, textbooks, magazines and journals, in notices at health centres, dentists' waiting rooms, libraries, on road signs and so on.

### Features of informative writing

Many types of informative writing have features in common. These may include:

- declarative sentences
- technical or specialist terminology
- objective writing
- abbreviations
- figures and diagrams
- headings and subheadings
- quotations
- numbered or bullet points
- a formal tone

**ACTIVITY 21**

In groups, think of pieces of informative writing that you are familiar with, and identify at least one of each of the listed features associated with this type of writing.

## Writing for a number of purposes

Although different purposes of writing tend to make use of different features and devices, it is not true that all pieces of writing of a certain type use the same techniques. Read the following piece of informative writing about a new music player. Although the writer provides information about the machine he is also expressing an opinion about it.

### TINY WALKMAN THAT TURNS YOUR COMPUTER INTO A RECORD STORE

IT WEIGHS less than three ounces, fits into the palm of a hand and is threatening to consign the CD, cassette tape and possibly even the music store, to history.

Electronics giant Sony yesterday unveiled the MS Walkman, the latest stage in the seemingly unstoppable technological advancement of music listening.

In the future, fans will no longer need to pop down to the high street to buy the latest releases. Instead, they will simply download them from the Internet . . .

#### THE SYSTEM

1   Download music from Internet on to home PC
2   Plug Walkman into PC and transfer music to it
3   Music is held digitally on tiny thumb-sized card inside unit
4   Play through headphones or speakers

#### THE PLAYER

1   *Memory*: Up to 2 hours of music
2   *Battery*: Four hours of continuous play
3   *Size*: approx 3.8″ tall; fits into palm
4   *Weight*: 2.4 oz, about same as small bar of chocolate . . .

## ACTIVITY 22 C3.2

Compare the informative features used in the article with the features itemised on page 128, and note their effects. Which of the features in the list were unsuitable for this writer's purpose?

Identify the language features in the article that you would not normally associate with informative writing. Why do you think the writer has employed them? And what do you think is the main purpose of this article?

Now read the commentary on pages 149–150.

## ACTIVITY 23 C3.3, LP3.2, LP3.3

Think of an invention that you are enthusiastic about. Write a short article giving basic information about it. Your primary purpose is to inform people about it – what it does, how it works, and so on – but you also want to make people keen in it. Identify the techniques you will need for each purpose.

Think about what facts you will include and how you will present them in a positive way. Ask your partner or group for feedback on your first draft, and redraft your material accordingly. How difficult was it to write for two purposes simultaneously?

## Writing for different audiences

One way of approaching the informative aspect of original writing is to take an already existing document and to re-present the information for a different audience. The next two passages provide information on the same subject area and both contain roughly the same information, but the audience for the second is younger than that for the first.

### VIKING

Also called NORSEMAN, or NORTHMAN, member of the Scandinavian seafaring warriors who raided and colonised wide areas of Europe from the 9th to the 11th century and whose disruptive influence profoundly affected European history. These pagan Danish, Norwegian, and Swedish warriors were probably prompted to undertake their raids by a combination of factors ranging from overpopulation at home to the relative helplessness of victims abroad.

The Vikings were made up of land-owning chieftains and clan heads, their retainers, freemen, and any energetic young clan members who sought adventure and booty overseas. At home these Scandinavians were independent farmers, but at sea they were raiders and pillagers. During the Viking period the Scandinavian countries seem to have possessed a practically inexhaustible surplus of manpower, and leaders of ability, who could organise groups of warriors into conquering bands and armies, were seldom lacking. These bands would negotiate the seas in their longships and mount hit-and-run raids at cities and towns along the coasts of Europe. Their burning, plundering, and killing earned them the name *vikingr*, meaning 'pirate' in the early Scandinavian languages.

## THE NORTHMEN

In the late 700s the former Anglo-Saxon pirates, now settled in England, the land they had made their own, received the first of a series of shocks – raids by the Northmen, pirates from Scandinavia. These Northmen were known as *Vikings*, from a Norse word meaning pirate. The monks who wrote the *Anglo-Saxon Chronicle* referred to them as 'the heathen' or 'the force'.

The Vikings were bold warriors, fierce and cruel. They sailed in longships, graceful vessels each of which carried a square sail and oars to cope with all weathers. They were well disciplined and loyal to one another. But in their raids they slaughtered, burned and robbed. They carried off all the most beautiful women, and took men to sell as slaves. In their churches the Saxons prayed: 'from the fury of the Norsemen, good Lord deliver us'.

## ACTIVITY 24

Identify the main pieces of information that the two passages share. What indications, if any, are there that the first extract assumes a more educated readership? Apart from vocabulary, what has had to be changed for the younger readers?

Now read the commentary on page 150.

When re-presenting information for a younger audience you should ask the following questions:

- How much of the detail in the original do you need, and how much is appropriate for your chosen audience?

- How much do your readers know about the subject, and how much do they need to know?

- Do you need to simplify any of the vocabulary or explain any terms?

- Do you need to simplify any concepts and/or explain them?

- What sentence structure is most suitable?

- How can the graphology of the text be altered to suit the needs of a younger audience?

Making use of your own subject expertise or personal interests, produce an informative booklet for use in year 7 classes. For example, you could write a brief outline of the life and works of a famous artist, writer, scientist or explorer, or an introduction to the orchestra or to a sport (its history, famous players and so on).

For this activity you will find it useful to collect examples of informative leaflets from such sources as libraries, health centres and tourist information offices. Make use of what you discover from your investigation of these texts. Think about your choice of vocabulary, the way the sentences need to be structured, the amount and type of information needed. You should also consider the use of pictures and images carefully, and a suitable layout.

# Writing to instruct and advise

As with the other purposes of writing we have looked at, texts with instruction as their primary purpose often make use of a number of specific techniques. However, as before, it would be wrong to imply that all instructional writing has to make use of these features – to do so would make the writing formulaic and ineffective. Before we look at how writers can adapt techniques and features for their own particular purposes and audiences, it will be useful to identify those features that commonly appear in this type of writing.

## Features of instructional writing

You will be familiar with many of the features of this type of writing from your work at GCSE. Here is a summary of the techniques and features often used in instructional writing:

- use of numbers, weights, measurements etc., to add precision

- use of abbreviations, such as 'k1, p1, k2tog, wfwd, k1, sl 1, p1, psso'.

- specialist terms, with or without definitions (depending on the audience)

- imperative verb forms – 'stir the mixture until it is smooth'

- simple sentences

- question and answer format

- use of subheadings

- numbered or bullet points for sequencing

- 'if . . . then' constructions

Read the following text, which is aimed at students and deals with how to avoid being mugged. You will find that although he uses some of the features mentioned above, the writer of this piece adapts them to suit his own purposes. What are those purposes?

# DAYLIGHT ROBBERS

No SOONER is the loan in your pocket than someone tries to steal it. Prepare yourself with Mark McDowall's anti-mugging plan.

Increasingly, students are prey to maniacs and subversives who leap out of the shadows making unreasonable demands for money, credit cards or a point of view. Don't give in, stun your adversary instead using one of our top tips:

1. If you are attacked, one thing you have on your side is the law. Follow the example of MP Alan Duncan, aide to Brian 'like the designer jacket' Mawhinney, and make a citizen's arrest. The assailant will stop, declare a fair cop and wait patiently until the police arrive. This could take up to 20 minutes, however, as the police, pissing themselves at the station, will find it hard to get their act together. . . .

7. Mastering the art of origami is easier than self-defence but no less effective. Divert the attention of your adversary with a mesmerising display of this ancient Chinese art-form. Emitting a series of low and unusual noises will add an air of intimidation to your display of this otherwise delightful pastime . . . .

12. Remember, wherever you are, you can always ring the Cone Hotline (01345 504030). Anyone noticing you do this, of course, will consider you a complete prat and leave you well alone.

13. If all else fails, try this: hand over your overdraft in its entirety and run.

## ACTIVITY 26

Identify which of the features of instructional writing listed on page 132 are used in this extract. Try to describe the tone of the piece, and its attitude to the audience and subject matter. Do you think the article is successful in appealing to its target audience ('freshers' at university)? If so, how does it achieve that appeal? What is the primary purpose of this piece of writing?

Now read the commentary on page 150.

## Adapting form for effect

A lot of your work in this module has been devoted to identifying features of different purposes of writing, showing an awareness of the readership, and understanding the conventions of the genre within which you are writing. Quite often there is a tension between these three. A writer may wish to adapt the features usually associated with a specific purpose of writing in order to meet the demands of a particular readership and genre.

The following extract is a piece of instructional writing from a women's magazine. The language of women's magazines has particular conventions, such as an informality of style; and the use of modern, young slang, colloquial expressions, tag questions and elision (normally associated with speech); and an assumption of particular values. The writer of articles for the magazine has to conform to the expectations of the reader as well as fulfil their own purposes – in this case to offer advice on earning more money.

# HOW TO EARN AS MUCH AS A MAN

Okay, the bottom line is, blokes earn more than women, full stop. How sick does that make you feel? How fuming, spitting furious, fit-to-bust frustrated? It's a galling thought, isn't it – that however hard you work, however determined you are to scale the company ladder, you're financially fated to take less home than him. What's weird is that we women have been led to believe that the work had been done for us – after all, equal pay laws were passed three decades ago. But it's a myth. According to a recent study, women still trail behind, earning on average 25% less than men for the same work. That's the bad news. Now for the good. You don't have to put up with it. We asked ten top-earning women to share their fat salary secrets with us. So read on and start raking it in. . . .

## IF YOU WANT IT, ASK FOR IT

says Leah Riches, 27, who owns her own company, INPHO PR, and bags £50,000 a year. After all, how many times have you settled for less than you deserve because you didn't want to rock the boat? Women are often afraid of looking greedy if they ask for a pay rise. Men, on the other hand, tend to be good at clawing extra dosh from their bosses. They know they have to push their luck to get a decent salary.

'I've learned to be a tough negotiator', says Leah. 'There are more women in the music industry now, but it's still male-dominated. I had a shock a few years ago when I found out a guy who was handling the same band was paid more than me. We were both freelance – he'd simply asked for more money. It might sound grabby, but if you don't ask, you don't get'

## ACTIVITY 27

Work out how much actual advice and instruction is given in this piece of writing. Who seems to be the target audience, and what is it about the language that indicates this particular group? Give examples and explain how they work in the extract.

Read the commentary on page 151.

Now you are going to write two pieces of instructional writing. Both will be instructions for the same thing, but they will differ according to the intended readership and the form in which they are to appear.

## ACTIVITY 28 | C3.1A, C3.3, LP3.2, LP3.3

First think of the subject of your instructions. This could be humorous or serious – an activity or a way of improving your life. Some suggestions are: coping with a job and looking after the house; how to survive a part-time job and study; how to train a dog to jump through hoops; how to organise a party; how to look after children in a playground . . . .

Now decide on the two forms in which you are going to write (for example, one a magazine article and the other a government leaflet). Be clear about the audience for each piece of writing (for example, men and women, old and young, educated and uneducated . . .).

Make notes for each form of writing under the following headings: lexical choices, grammatical choice, graphology choices, tone and relationship with audience.

Now write each piece and get feedback from the other members of your group. Remember to keep all your notes and drafts for your coursework folder.

## Writing about writing: the commentary

In this module, you have looked at various different types of writing that you could produce for your coursework assignments. You must remember, however, that each piece of coursework has to be accompanied by a commentary. Forty per cent of the marks available in this module are given for the commentary. It is important that you spend time working on this, making sure that you give an accurate account of the writing you have done and the choices you have made.

The syllabus requirements for the commentary are that it should adopt a form that permits you to analyse and review:

- your choice of vocabulary and syntactic structures

- your style of writing

- the overall structure and organisation of your text

- any changes made during drafting and re-drafting

This is the part of your coursework where all the notes you have made about your own and other writers' work are going to be very useful. The work you have done in examining the style and techniques used in the various genres covered in this book will help you in the production of your own writing, and should also contribute significantly to your ability to discuss your own techniques and the process of writing itself.

If you followed our advice and kept detailed notes on the planning processes for all your original writing tasks, then you should be able to write about the origins of any piece – where you got the idea – and how you got started in terms of preparatory work. Here are some other questions that should help you to compile your commentary:

- Did you need to do any background reading or interviews?

- Did you model your work on any particular style or format?

- Who is the audience for your piece of work?

- Did you sample any reactions to your writing?

- What was the response of the intended readership?

- Did you get any other feedback?

- Did you make any changes as a result of feedback – or for any other reason?

- How did you decide on the lexis, tone and level of formality to adopt?

- Did you have to adapt this at any point and if so, why?

- How have you structured and organised your work?

- How successful do you feel you have been in producing the particular style?

- Have you compared your finished piece with any published work of the same type?

Try to avoid making vague comments. Always be precise and give examples from your piece of writing which relate to the point being made. On the other hand, avoid giving a narrative account of the content of your work. You must provide detailed information about the processes you went through in planning, redrafting and polishing your work. If you refer to the list of questions above you should be able to avoid the narrative approach. Once again, this is the stage at which you will find your own notes from class exercises most useful.

Finally, try to avoid being long-winded about your inspiration for the piece. The examiner does not want a life history or a third piece of original writing.

## Examples from student commentaries

Here are a number of extracts reproduced from other students' commentaries. They should help you to get an idea of the kind of work that is expected from this part of the coursework. The first is a short extract from a very detailed student commentary that appeared under the heading 'Formulating my ideas'.

I decided to write a short guide to group planning on a day unit. The piece would be aimed at new staff members that now work in my place, and would present helpful ways of approaching group planning.

To ensure that I was aiming at a 'gap in the market' I visited my old work place and spoke to staff members. Senior staff members confirmed that they did not have a simple guide of this nature that could be easily referred to.

Here the student has indicated what type of background research was carried out, and that the piece will fulfil a perceived need. Elsewhere in the commentary, the student also referred to research into other pieces of informative writing:

Points I noticed were the importance of clear titles or headings and the use of paragraphs as a means of separating information into meaningful and possibly more accessible sections. Some information was highlighted to show its importance as a key point or act as a kind of signpost, indicating the general subject area of a paragraph or section. At times the highlighted words were mid-paragraph, at other times titles or straplines were highlighted.

The student has again shown that they undertook relevant background reading and research and understood the functions of relevant techniques. This extract is only a section from the part of the commentary that relates to background reading.

The next extract concerns the feedback the student received.

Staff felt I had achieved what I had set out to do, and asked if they could have copies of the guide.

I asked a senior staff member who had been responsible for my training during my period working on the unit to read the guide to ensure all my information was correct.

She told me everything was fine – much to my relief! She also asked if it would be possible to use the guide for training purposes.

This student has been thorough, both in the writing of the commentary and in the construction and preparation of the piece itself.

Here is an extract from another student's commentary, this time dealing with language choices – in this case semantic fields:

All the way through the piece I have used certain semantic fields that are common with the tabloid style of writing. Firstly, and most obviously, I have used the semantic field of football with terms like 'man of the match', 'cup tie', 'midfield' and 'striker' that are widely associated with football.

I have also written using the semantic field of war and creating the image that the football game was a battle. I have done this by using terms such as 'General Vialli', 'stepped into battle', 'drew first blood', 'battle royal' and 'ten troops'. All of these terms suggest images of war and fighting and help to emphasise how fierce the competition was in a way that is familiar to those reading the piece.

Here the student has shown that when writing the piece they were consciously aware of the effects created by their language choices. In the opening sentence the student also indicates an awareness of the techniques used in models – in this case tabloid sports reports.

There now follows a complete commentary for a piece of student coursework. First read the extract from the coursework itself, then the accompanying commentary that follows it.

## HOW TO BE FAMOUS

No matter who it is, or what they do, every person in the country strives to be famous and, although to the naked eye it may not seem so, success and fame in any area is simple. No really, and there are many examples to prove this true. So, whatever career you desire to make it 'big' in, just sit back and follow the easy guidelines for the fame of your choice and you'll be barfing with Baker and guzzling with Gazza before you can say 'Chris Evans is as cool as a Christmas cracker'.

### HOW TO MAKE IT IN MUSIC

. . . if you're still a little down-hearted, then don't worry, because there is, amazingly, still a lot more hope. Don't forget that in the business of making music you really don't have to be an 'oil painting' as it might be said. However, don't forget that if your looks aren't your greatest asset then an attitude, an outrageous side or, even better, both can really help pop up your prospects. If you don't believe me just take a look at the example of the original bad boys of British music, The Rolling Stones. Possibly the ugliest group of men ever to appear in the public eye started their very own, very nasty and popular movement that has captured audiences for the best part of a century and created the biggest rock and roll phenomenon ever. . . allegedly. And it's still going!

### HOW TO MAKE IT IN TV

Don't worry if you are unfortunate enough to have a strong tendency to annoy people, as in certain cases this can be an advantage and, in fact, for some people the more intolerable they are the more popular they get. Just take a look at two recent examples:

1. Jeremy Beadle. Enough said.

2. Chris Evans. The original ginger whinger has infuriated so many people that he's now a multi-millionaire and at the top of his profession. Just keep it in mind, this could be a good one.

## . . . Now finally . . .

If you've scraped past on the previous four pointers then you need just one more thing, and the most important of all, to launch yourself into the world of television. You must remember that in general in TV you DO have to be attractive to the audience. Only the odd exceptions to this rule slip through the control gates and research shows they don't get very far. So if you are attractively challenged it's goodbye to TV.

NOTE: it is possible to avoid this rule. If you happen to become famous in another field you can, later in life, try to lose all dignity in an attempt to boost your retirement fund by becoming an expert in your field when your time is up there. This is a very popular path for sports persons to take.

## Student's commentary on 'How to be famous'

This piece of writing is primarily written for entertainment but has a slight twist in the fact that it is written in the style of an instructional piece. I came up with the idea because I did not want to write a typical entertainment piece in the style of a story or something similar. I wanted to do something different so that it would be more fun for me to write and also more fun for people to read. I decided that I wanted to write the piece about music because it is something that I am particularly interested in and enjoy so the piece began as: 'How to Make it in Music'. However, while writing I realised that the music idea would not make the piece as long as I had hoped and so, instead of getting rid of what I saw as a good idea, I came up with the idea to change the theme of the piece to 'How to be Famous' and I added television and radio to the piece.

The audience for this piece is teenagers who are aged from around thirteen to eighteen and are both male and female. I pictured the piece being in a teen magazine for both boys and girls so in writing the piece I tried to get a cross between the types of writing in magazines like 'Loaded' and 'FHM' and the writing styles in magazines like 'Bliss' and 'Just Seventeen'. I got my broad idea of how to write with this crossover of styles by looking at the various styles of writing in my magazines and the magazines owned by my sister. Because of the intended audience and the type of magazine it would be in the piece is informal and so I have used non-standard grammar, vocabulary and slang on several occasions.

This is the third and final draft of this piece and I have made changes from the second draft. In general the changes were corrections of spelling and punctuation. The only significant change is I have re-worded the final sentence in the first paragraph to make it more tidy and to make it sound better. The changes that I have made came after I asked friends of mine to read the piece and then give me their honest opinions about it. I feel that these changes and the ones made for previous drafts have definitely improved the piece and I feel that this final draft is as good as I can make the piece as I feel that it will have a better impact on the reader in its current form than it would if it differed in any way.

The piece is written as instructions to the reader but the instructions are full of humour and irony which gives the piece an interesting twist and makes it entertaining. Because of the intentions and style of the piece I have used a very lighthearted tone. As the piece is written as a set of instructions I have used bullet points throughout to denote the start of each new instruction. I feel that the theme of the piece goes well with the style of teen magazines as they often include 'How to . . .' sections and they are usually in a lighthearted manner that has insults aimed at the subject which is exactly what I have done. Also, my piece talks about those people in the public eye as does just about every teen magazine going.

I have used many different grammatical techniques in writing this piece to install the lighthearted tone and humour throughout the piece. The main grammatical technique that I have used is alliteration as I feel that it is an excellent device for creating and emphasising humour as well as making the piece more interesting to read. Some of the main examples of this are 'captivating chord patterns' which is an ironic insult at the actual dullness, 'total tone deafness' and 'sordid singing' which both emphasise the inabilities of a particular group in an amusing way.

Another way in which I have created humour is by beginning a sentence, stopping part of the way through it and then correcting myself while rephrasing the sentence. One example of this is: 'The biggest rock and roll phenomenon ever . . . allegedly'. This creates humour by poking fun at political correctness and some of the other examples poke fun at the strange terms used by famous people.

To create fun, humour and excitement I have used the phonology of particular words in two different ways. Firstly, I have used rhyme to emphasise the humour and irony in certain points. One example of this use of rhyme is 'ginger whinger' which insults a particular person in a way that would be familiar and amusing to teens. The other way that I have used the phonology to good effect is by using parallel structures to give the piece a good feel and flow and thus make it better for people to read. The main example of this use of parallel structures is 'barfing with Baker' and 'guzzling with Gazza' right next to each other which creates a nice sound as both statements have the same pattern of words and the numbers of syllables in those words.

One technique that I have used to provoke the reader's imagination and once again to create humour is using similes in the normal way and also using paradoxical similes to put great emphasis on humour. An example of a normal simile, but with a famous twist that I have used is when I have written that someone 'loses popularity as fast as a Man. Utd Team without a trophy'. Here I am making a joke at the expense of a football team and so this implies previous knowledge. The paradoxical similes that I have used are primarily aimed at adding to the humour of the piece. One example of this type of simile is where I have written 'Chris Evans is as cool as a Christmas cracker'. Here I have moved away from the traditional simile to create humour and with the addition of alliteration this adds together to create a rather emphatic and amusing statement.

In the middle of the piece, at the end of the music section, I have written a quick fame warning that is deliberately elliptical as the wording gives the impression that the warning is serious and is like the kind of warning found on appliance packages. This kind of a notice will be familiar to teens from computer and stereo packaging and will seem funny to the audience because of this.

The final thing that I have done to make this piece more like other pieces of similar styles and to make it more appropriate for the audience is including slang and non-standard terms that will be understood by teens. Examples of these words are 'whinger', 'cool', 'TV' and 'showbiz' which are all terms which are familiar to teens and thus make the piece more welcoming to the audience. As well as this I have abbreviated all the sets of words like 'do not' and 'you have' to 'don't' and 'you've' because I feel that this is more in tune with the speech and writing of teens and the lack of abbreviations like this was one of the failures of the first drafts.

The change of 'do not' to 'don't' and other similar abbreviations were the final improvements that I feel I needed to make it as good as it can be. I am now very happy with this final draft, I feel that the humour and irony are just right and I also think that the intentional bluntness and scathing insults in some parts work well for the piece and fit in well with the tone of the piece as these kinds of amusing insults are common in teen magazines as it is a kind of reassurance that the famous are not all high and mighty. In all I feel that the piece would now fit in a teen mag extremely well and is as good as I can make it.

## ACTIVITY 29

Has the student effectively described how they came to write the piece? Is the target audience specified and, if so, do you think it is accurately identified and described? (You will need to refer to the original piece of work here.) Decide whether the student has described and accounted for any changes they made, and more generally whether you found the comments useful. What changes would you make, if any, to improve the clarity of the commentary?

You have not been given the original piece of coursework in its entirety, but you have enough to compare what the student says in the commentary about style and content with the extract itself. What, if anything, would you add to the commentary?

## Organising your coursework folder

Your coursework folder needs to be accessible to both your teacher and the moderator. They must be able to find their way through your work relatively easily. It is in your best interests to have a system of organisation that facilitates the marking of your work.

Have a table of contents, and number your pages; ensure that you give the correct page references in the contents. Provide a bibliography for each piece of work, stating precisely which sources – books, pamphlets, websites, etc. – you used. If you used pamphlets or newspaper articles, it is best to include the originals with your work. Use dividers of some sort to mark off the different sections of your work, and label them. Give accurate word-counts for each piece of work.

Here are two alternative sequences for organising your coursework folder. Whichever you choose, you should remember to be both consistent and organised.

## System 1

This approach keeps each piece of writing together with its own commentary, drafts and supporting materials. Place the final draft of each piece of work at the beginning of each section, followed by the final commentary. Place the bibliography and any source material after this. This should be followed in each case by all your rough work and draft copies. Your folder will then look something like this:

- table of contents

- cover sheet for first piece of work

- final draft of first piece

- final commentary for first piece

- bibliography

- cover sheet for rough work

- drafts and rough work for first piece

- cover sheet for second piece of work

- final draft of second piece

- final commentary for second piece

- bibliography

- cover sheet for rough work

- drafts and rough work for second piece

## System 2

Another way of organising your folder is to separate the written pieces, commentaries and draft/rough materials into their own sections, so the sequence could be:

- table of contents

- cover sheet for final draft of first piece of work

- final draft of first piece

- bibliography

- cover sheet for final draft of second piece of work

- final draft of second piece

- bibliography

- cover sheet for commentaries

- commentary for both pieces

- cover sheet for drafts and rough work for first piece

- rough work and drafts for first piece

- cover sheet for drafts and rough work for second piece

- rough work and drafts for second piece

Both of these approaches are suggestions only, but it is in your own interests to organise your work in such a way that the people who are marking it can quickly find the work which they are supposed to be marking.

# Commentaries

## Activity 1

The title of the article makes implicit reference to the title of a film – *Blazing Saddles* – and to a series of books for children by Enid Blyton – the 'Famous Five' series. The reference to the children's programme *Mr Benn* continues this assumption of a shared cultural background and perhaps gives some indication of the presumed age of the readership. *Mr Benn* and *Blazing Saddles* might not be immediately obvious references to an audience much under the age of thirty. Captain Birdseye would probably not pose any difficulty for a younger audience, though, despite the fact that he has been around for a long time.

The 'laddish' feel of the article is increased through the references to beer drinking and football as 'pastimes'. The readers of the magazine in which this article appeared would probably have expected this laddish approach, which continues with the way in which the Irish 'Joe' is described, using stereotypical references to 'a bog full of peat' (large areas of Ireland are peat bog); 'a tin whistle' (a musical instrument associated with Irish folk music); and a 'pint-a Arrrp' (Harp lager, brewed in Ireland).

The writer makes use of some interesting figurative language to describe the weather and the sensation of cycling at speed downhill: 'sadly souped in fog' is both alliterative and figurative, making use of the old expression for a thick fog – a pea-souper. This expression creates an image of physical discomfort and of entrapment at the same time. The unexpected downward movement is captured in the expression 'God tilts a hill downwards', the use of the present tense enhances the suddenness of the downward movement, and the reference to God is perhaps appropriate in this rather irreverent look at Ireland – a country renowned for its Catholicism.

The 'freewheel adrenaline of landscape rush' encapsulates a description of the effect, both physical and mental, of the sudden downward motion. The 'rush' is felt as that of the landscape and not of the cyclist; this describes, very economically, the feeling of cycling downhill at speed – it is not you who seems to be moving but the scenery. Describing the ride as 'a bumpy, butt-hammering 30-mile-an-hour trip' is not only alliterative but almost onomatopoeic, giving the impression, very graphically, of an uncomfortable ride.

The writer has managed to create the impression of being a somewhat less than enthusiastic participant in this holiday. It is not his 'thing', or not the sort of thing that he would normally be associated with. There is humour in this extract and a sense of 'place', although they are affected by the writer's opinion. He strikes the pose of someone who is usually far too sophisticated to enjoy this type of holiday, and yet the way in which he writes indicates that perhaps he enjoyed it more than he would like to admit.

## Activity 3

Obviously, anyone could read and enjoy this text. However, it seems likely that Sue Townsend had a teenage audience in mind when she wrote it. The subject matter of the extract contains references to things that would concern a teenager: skin problems, diet, the contrast between a mother and a grandmother in terms of attitude towards the diary writer, comments upon the mother's attitude and that of the family doctor. All of these could imply the inclusion of a younger audience but would not exclude an older one.

The final sentence of the entry 'But frankly, my dear diary, I don't give a damn' might not be recognised by younger readers as a reference to the film *Gone with the Wind*, which was filmed in the late 1930s. Yet this type of obscure reference might be consistent with the character of the writer of the diary.

The first sentence is elliptical – the word 'I' is not used and this is associated with brief diary entries. The lexis is not unusual for a 14-year-old, being a mixture of the relatively sophisticated 'inadequate' and the more informal 'boil-in-the-bag stuff'.

The writer of the diary takes himself and his ailments seriously. References to his 'inadequate' diet, the possibility of an 'allergy' to plastic, his 'nourishment' and to 'lassa fever' all support this view. He feels very sorry for himself, something emphasised by his use of exclamation marks and the rhetorical question 'Surely her child should come before her job?' The sentence 'It is very clean and peaceful' contains an implied criticism of his own home; presumably he believes that it is the opposite.

Despite the fact that he takes himself so seriously, there is an amusing feel to this extract. This is because the author who created this character has taken so many of the complaints that children make about their parents and given them to someone who exaggerates them to the point where we cannot take them seriously.

## Activity 4

The extract is taken from an epistolary novel set in the United States.

*Lexis and grammar.* You could have noticed any of the following things about the lexis and grammar of the text. It uses words and expressions more commonly associated with everyday spoken language, such as 'never had a kine word' and 'to see after'. Lexis is simple and almost totally monosyllabic. Non-standard grammar is used – for example, the past tense is not always used, as in 'after little Lucious come', 'he leave her alone', and 'A week go by'. Sentences are simple and, on the whole, short. The italicised words at the beginning contain a double negative.

*Graphology.* You could have noticed any of the following things about the graphology of this text. The letter is preceded by two sentences written in italic and separated by white space from the rest of the text. Direct speech is not signalled through the use of speech marks. The words 'I am' have been crossed out and replaced by 'I have always been'.

*Character.* All of this linguistic evidence can lead up to the following assumptions about the character in this extract:

- The writer of the letter is a young, relatively uneducated, girl who is being sexually abused by her mother's husband. The opening words are not those of the letter writer and give us some clues as to why she is writing to God. Their inclusion indicates a stylistic sophistication that is at odds with the actual style of the letter.

- The writer feels alone, isolated and afraid. She is ignorant about what is happening to her and uncertain about her own guilt: 'I am' has been replaced by 'I have always been'.

The non-punctuation of speech and the way that words are spelled as they might be pronounced is some indication of the writer's educational level. (It is not only when she is quoting others that she does this – for example, 'kine'.)

Elements of graphology, lexis and grammar indicate that the writer is American: 'I ain't', 'Naw', 'kine', 'he leave her alone', 'an all these chilren'. The non-marking for possession – 'sister doctor' – which is a characteristic of Black American English might lead us to make a further assumption about the writer of the letter. Events are presented baldly and as if the writer were speaking directly to another person, relating events which have led to her confusion: 'Maybe you can give me a sign letting me know what is happening to me'.

Although this is written in letter form, because it is addressed to God perhaps we ought to see it as closer to a form of journal or diary. After all, the letters are never going to be sent!

You can see from this brief analysis the ways in which the author, who is not to be confused with the (fictional) writer of the letter, has introduced a sympathetic character, a situation and possibly a setting too.

## Activity 8

The male character is presented as hard, cold, someone to be feared. Lexis that suggests this includes: 'craggy' suggesting hard rocks, 'the hard angle of his jaw', 'the glacier coldness of his eyes'( which is mentioned three times in this short passage) and the fact that the woman felt 'a tingle of fear' at the thought of 'the strength he exuded'. Of course, despite the third person narrative this is still the viewpoint of the woman and tells us something of what she finds attractive in a man.

The descriptions of his physical attributes are again as suggestive of the woman's attraction as they are of the actual appearance of the man. His height is stressed – 'tall, taller . . . towering' – as is his athleticism – 'like a well-honed athlete', 'halfback shoulders', 'flat stomach, trim hips and powerful thighs'. The descriptions and her responses are all sexually suggestive: 'Fearing she would be caught staring where she shouldn't, Alison kept her eyes pinned above the waist'. Her responses are equally suggestive: the 'tingle of fear', 'She took a sudden breath', she was 'robbed . . . of her breath' and she 'felt warm all over'. She is described as being 'further captivated', implying that she has already been entranced or held captive by him.

In this short extract we can already see the contrast built in to the title – the warmth of her response to him contrasted with the perceived coldness in him. The title of the series, 'Silhouette Desire', leaves little to the prospective reader's imagination and this passage would not disappoint, with its indications of strong physical attraction mingled with fear.

## Activity 10

In terms of content, the Dahl version omits the whole of the introductory, rather romantic explanation of how Snow White was named and begins instead, with the abrupt opening 'When little Snow-White's mother died'. The abruptness is continued through the use of the exclamatory speech of the king. The spoken word is an important area of this version, and Dahl has introduced more speech than was in the original. It is in the words given to the characters that a good deal of the humour lies. For instance instead of the formulaic and formal responses of the looking-glass, we have the use of idiomatic expressions (Queen, you are the cat's pyjamas) and slang (scrag). This is consistent throughout; the king is described as having a 'shifty' smile and the queen says 'I'll skin 'er'. The rhyme and rhythm of the poem are important. Each line has eight syllables, four of which are stressed. This creates a regular and rather 'jog-trot' rhythm appropriate to the humorous content. The rhyming is in the form of rhyming couplets (pairs of lines rhyme) and the rhymed words take the final stress of the line. The regularity of the rhythm and rhyme make the piece ideal for reading aloud and the colloquial, iodiomatic and humorous language encourage the reader to add expression when reading. A dramatic effect is created.

## Activity 12

*Waitress*: here, the 'original' word is waiter. The addition of the diminutive '-ess' can be seen as belittling to women. Similar forms are: major–majorette (a small major?); actor-actress (often, now, women who act refer to themselves as actors in the same way that, to avoid inbuilt bias, female sculptors avoid the label 'sculptress').

*Old-age pensioner*: the term can be seen as insulting to that group of people now usually referred to as 'senior citizens' or simply as 'pensioners'. The age bias built in to the expression is offensive, and could be taken to imply that the people to whom it applies are somehow deficient.

*Disabled*: the preferred nomination is now often 'differently abled'. This is a controversial area, as even those to whom the 'label' applies disagress as to the correct terminology; 'disabled' seems to imply that the person to whom it applies is 'unable' to do anything.

*Chairman*: this is one of those words that some would argue makes use of the generic 'he'. Merely because 'man' is used this does not exclude women. Others might argue that the very use of 'man' in this context implies that only men can be 'in charge'. There are all sorts of problems relating to this particular usage and its alternatives – some women object to the use of 'chairwoman' when the presiding person is a women and prefer the alternatives 'chairperson' or simply 'chair'.

## Activity 15

The main thrust of this piece would seem to be that when it comes to the eating habits of other nations we ought perhaps to live and let live. The South Koreans, it is suggested, might have left their menus intact.

The audience is, most obviously, readers of the *Guardian*, a newspaper that in general adopts a liberal approach. The writer can assume that the audience will, at least to some extent, take the same liberal and perhaps slightly cynical view. A piece on the same subject in, say, the *Sun* would probably have highlighted the 'dog menus' in a much more sensational way, and appealed to its readership's sentimentalism.

The writer uses humour in '"puppy fat" conceals saucy delights' and the sentence that ends the second paragraph, 'This is sensitive stuff'. The piece pokes gentle fun at the way the British view the dog, which is discussed in the first paragraph.

There is a three-part structure to the piece: the first paragraph talks about the relationship of the English and their dogs; the second paragraph discusses the relationship of the South Koreans and their dogs and also introduces the point at issue, the continued ban on dog meat; and the third and final paragraph raises a series of questions about our attitude towards the eating habits of other nations.

The writer also makes a final point about the state of British football: 'our national teams have gone to the dogs'. This is not the only idiomatic expression used: the title has 'dog's dinner', and we also find 'four-legged friend'. Perhaps the idea behind this final point is that the whole thing is not worth getting in a stew about; the English football team is so bad that supporters will not be going to Korea.

## Activity 17

There is a very personal feel to this piece of writing; it creates a sense that the writer is speaking to friends who are familiar with his viewpoints and manner of expression. This effect is created in the first place by the use of direct address. The very first word of the article is 'You'. The reader is involved from the outset. The second paragraph answers an assumed question posed by the readership. This paragraph assumes that the reader is familiar with the writer's views on some animal 'welfare' groups (not necessarily the RSPCA), though here you can see that he doesn't think they are acting in the best interests of animals. The use of inverted commas is here an indication of irony.

Further into the article he poses another rhetorical question: 'Think old Gunner has lost his marbles, do you?' As with the first question, this uses an idiomatic expression: 'lost his marbles'. The first question used 'never thought you'd see the day', and later in the piece we find 'spanner in the works'. These are all expressions that the writer probably assumes his readers use themselves, and this contributes to the sense of familiarity. There is an assumption throughout that the reader, like old Gunner (whose pen name says a good deal), 'rides to hounds' or hunts in some way.

There is some humour in 'Cats, you see, are not politically incorrect'. The implication here is that hounds *are* politically incorrect. The description of the cats as a pack of hounds would add to the humour for his readership, who would be used to seeing the activities of their own hounds described in this way. However, the writer has a very serious point to make, and this description does introduce it. He contrasts the way the cats will be released to kill with the ways in which huntsmen have safeguards to ensure no animal suffers unduly. Here again he can probably assume the general support of his readership. The use of 'In fact' to start the third paragraph introduces this contrast. He doesn't need to spell out that his readers do something that the RSPCA will not; he offers an 'us and them' – 'we do this, they will not'.

The second half of the piece is less flippant and introduces the use of facts and figures to back up his point that cats are a threat to wildlife to a greater degree than hounds or hunting in general. He uses a quotation from a 'leading researcher' (note that the researcher is not named, so this cannot be verified). Facts, figures and 'expert opinion' are used to strengthen any piece of persuasive writing, from advertisements to political speeches. They give weight to the expression of a personal opinion, political viewpoint or a product's credibility. Together with the way that the second part of this article is written, including the use of emotive language ('kill wantonly'), these points help to ensure that the message is not lost on the reader.

The final sentence reverts to the tone of the first part of the article and reintroduces an element of humour. The writer has adopted what one feels is his customary approach to his reader. The relationship is re-established.

## Activity 19

The writer of the first review takes a rather cynical view of Lucas's motivation in producing another 'Star Wars' movie. The information about the film is contained in the three sentences beginning 'George Lucas's prequel . . .'. These sentences give a brief overview of the content and major characters and an evaluation of the special effects. The imperative structures in the review are used to reinforce the writer's view that money is the driving force: 'Buy the . . .'. This is consistent with the expressions such as 'cash cow' when referring to the 'Force' and adds to the cynicism of the tone. All of this is appropriate to the intended readership. Readers of *Marie Claire* would not be likely to expect a rave review of *Star Wars* films.

The review of *Wild, Wild West* has a very informal and 'chatty' tone that is appropriate for the type of magazine in which it appears. The writer has used a style of language closer to that of casual conversation – 'loadsa', 'sexy bum', 'give 'em'. Some of the adjectives used are informal, though not necessarily what readers would use themselves in speech – 'Funky', 'cheesy', 'weird and whacky', 'crackerjack'. Other devices used that would probably not be found in a review for an older audience include the use of elision – 'acting's cheesy', 'plot's paper-thin' – and the use of abbreviation – 'v. evil'.

Focusing upon the attributes of the popular Will Smith might make the film seem an attractive prospect. However, the writer describes the acting as 'cheesy' and the plot as 'paper-thin', which might persuade readers that the film was not worth seeing were it not for the final, positive description of the effects as 'crackerjack'.

## Activity 22

This is part of an informative article in which the writer's own interest is apparent. The first three short paragraphs are made up of declarative sentences, though these sentences are not merely factual but offer a view of a possible future for the music industry. Both 'threatening to consign . . . to history' and 'In the future' discuss possibilities. We also find in this piece the use of directives or imperatives, more usually associated with writing that instructs: 'Download music from Internet.' This use of directives allows the writer to present concisely detailed information about the working of the device and to stress its ease of use.

We do find technical terminology, but it is of a kind that most informed readers today will be familiar with, such as 'digitally', 'Download' and other terms associated with computers and music systems. There are also figures relating to size, weight and capacity – all providing essential information.

In the full article, which has not been reproduced here, headings and subheadings are used throughout to guide the reader. The two boxes containing numbered points serve to give prominence to the essential features of the system. They summarise, and because they are given physical prominence on the page, attract the attention of the casual reader who might not otherwise have read the article.

## Activity 24

Both passages contain an explanation of the name 'Viking' and inform the reader as to the nationality and exploits of the Vikings. Both inform the reader that the Northmen were pagan warriors who raided the coasts of Europe in their longships.

The first passage uses words and expressions which assume a more educated audience than the second. We find such things as: 'disruptive influence'; 'profoundly affected'; 'combination of factors'; and 'inexhaustible surplus of manpower'. In each of these cases it is not merely the lexis which a younger reader would find difficult, but the ideas. The first passage assumes a certain level of education in the reader so that ideas and concepts are introduced with no need for explanation. For instance, in the second passage there is a description of a longship which we do not find in the first, probably because it can be assumed that most adult readers would have this information. Other lexis has been simplified: 'would negotiate' becomes 'sailed'. Note the use of the modal 'would' in the first where the second uses the more straighforward past. This use of modals is found elsewhere in the first and not at all in the second. So we can also say that the grammar has been affected by the choice of audience.

## Activity 26

The primary purpose of this text seems to be to entertain, but there could be a serious purpose here. The article is aimed at young people who are newly independent and living away from home for the first time. Given this audience, the writer does not want to adopt a self-righteous tone or appear to be preaching.

The tone is flippant, bordering on being dismissive of the dangers, and most of the advice is obviously ridiculous. The writer pokes fun at the police – a traditional target for student jokes – and at such things as origami – no self-respecting student would admit to an interest in it. The coning of motorways and the 'Hotline' is also ridiculed.

Irony can be found in such things as the reference to origami as a 'delightful pastime'. Hyperbole appears in 'students are prey to maniacs and subversives'. These add to the humorous tone and, taken together with the references to political figures, assume a certain attitude to authority and some knowledge of current affairs.

## Activity 27

The only real piece of advice contained in this is that if a woman wants more money, then she must ask for it. Given the age and profession of the person quoted, the audience would seem to be young, professional women, who are in managerial positions or who aspire to management: independently minded young women.

Both the writer of the article and the person quoted use idiomatic and clichéd expressions. The writer uses the expressions 'bag', 'rock the boat' and 'push their luck', all more usually associated with speech. This use by the writer of colloquial expressions helps to give the piece as a whole some cohesion because the effect of the words in speech marks is also of spoken language. There is an informal tone to the passage and as it is based upon personal experience this is appropriate. The question in the first paragraph includes the reader within this special group of people who deserve more than they are receiving so that even if they are not in the fortunate position of Leah Riches, they perhaps feel that they could be.

The final, one-sentence paragraph gives the actual advice and this is given in a negative form '. . . if you don't ask, you don't get. This final sentence continues the informal approach and prevents the article as a whole from appearing to preach, something which one feels the assumed readership would not appreciate.

# Glossary

**Accent:** the pronunciation of language characteristic of a particular region or social group

**Adjacency pair:** a pair of 'turns' in a conversation, the basic unit of interactive talk

**Alliteration:** the repetition of similar (usually initial) consonant sounds in successive words

**Archaism:** language which is recognisably dated or which includes usage and meanings no longer current

**Assonance:** the repetition within successive words of similar vowel sounds

**Colloquialism:** literally, the language of speech; in practice, very informal uses of language

**Connotation:** not so much the surface meaning of a word as what it implies or suggests, e.g. 'home' = warmth, security, cosiness

**Convergence:** the tendency for speakers to reduce the differences in their speech to signal identification and belonging (see also Divergence)

**Covert prestige:** the unofficial or hidden prestige which a community attaches to a non-standard variety of the language (see Overt Prestige)

**Declarative:** the most common sentence type, a statement

**Deficit Model:** a view of non-standard (and children's) language which assumes they are inferior to standard, adult forms

**Dialect:** the distinctive vocabulary and grammatical constructions of a particular geographical area within a language community

**Discourse:** any extended passage of either spoken or written language

**Discourse structure:** the underlying pattern which a piece of discourse follows

**Divergence:** the tendency for speakers to exaggerate the differences in their speech to signal non-identification and distance (see also Convergence)

**Double/multiple negative:** the use of several negative markers in non-standard verb constructions such as 'You've never done nothing'

**Figurative language:** similes, metaphors and other non-literal uses of language

**Fillers:** elements of spoken language with little meaning, either verbal ('you know') or non-verbal ('er')

**Genre:** a recognisable type of text or discourse with characteristic elements or ingredients

**Graphology:** those features which contribute to the visual appearance of a text on the page

**Hedge:** in conversational analysis, a word or phrase which a speaker uses to indicate a degree of uncertainty or tentativeness

**Idiolect:** those distinctive features of a person's language which mark them out as an individual

**Idiom:** an expression whose meaning is unpredictable from the literal sense of its words, e.g. 'he fouled up big time'

**Imperative:** the command form of a verb or sentence

**Inflection:** an ending of a word which alters to indicate a change in grammatical meaning (e.g. -ed for past tense, -s for plurals)

**Interrogative:** the question form of a sentence

**Intonation:** the movement of the voice up and down in pitch during speech

**Lexis:** the collective term for the vocabulary of a language

**Lexical gap:** the apparent lack in a language of a word or phrase to express a particular meaning or idea

**Marking:** in grammar and semantics, the part of a word or phrase which explicitly identifies either a grammatical function (e.g. -ed for past tense) or other meaning (-ess for female in 'actress')

**Medium:** means of communnication (e.g. tv, radio, article, discussion, etc)

**Minimal response:** in conversational analysis, short utterences made in response to a speaker (such as 'yes', 'mm', 'I see')

**Onomatopoeia:** the phonetic imitation in language of actual sounds (e.g. buzz, pop)

**Orthography:** spelling and other aspects (e.g. punctuation) of the writing system

**Overt prestige:** the obvious and official high status attached to forms such as Standard English and Received Pronunciation (see also **Convert prestige**)

**Parallelism:** the successive repetition of similar phrase or sentence structures, a common rhetorical technique

**Paralinguistic features:** gestures and accompanying facial expressions which contribute to the communication of meanings in speech

**Person:** as in 1st (I, we) 2nd (you) and 3rd (s/he, they, it): a way of referring to the different possible subjects of a verb

**Phatic talk:** in conversational analysis, (small) talk whose primary function is to develop social relationships

**Phonemes:** the basic sounds (vowels and consonants) from which a language is built

**Prosodic features:** those aspects of the use of voice (intonation, stress, tempo, pitch) which contribute to meanings communicated in speech

**Phonology:** the study of those aspects of a language connected to its sounds

**Pun:** a deliberate play on two or more possible meanings of a word

**Question tag:** short question forms (such as 'isn't it?' and 'don't you?') 'tagged' onto the end of utterances

**Received Pronunciation (RP):** the 'neutral' accent of educated, professional speech

**Register:** the level of formality and topic-related vocabulary specific to a particular text

**Rhetoric:** the collective term for a range of linguistic techniques designed to move and persuade

**Rhetorical question:** a question which does not require an answer but is used persuasively

**Semantic field:** a grouping of words with related or similar meanings

**Sociolect:** the distinctive vocabulary and grammatical constructions particular to an identifiable social group

**Slang:** language which is not generally accepted as part of polite, Standard English (not to be confused with dialect)

**Standard English:** the accepted vocabulary and grammatical constructions of educated, 'correct' English

**Stress:** the emphasis placed on a particular word or syllable in speech

**Syntax:** that aspect of grammar concerned with the construction of sentences

**Taboo language:** language which is considered offensive (including swear words)

**Topic management:** in conversational analysis, the control exercised by speakers over what gets talked about

**Transcript:** an accurate written record of spoken discourse

**Triad/Triadic structure:** a three-part construction, either of discourse or sentence